MISSION IN
INDUSTRIAL FRANCE

Georges Velten

SCM PRESS LTD
LONDON

SBN 334 01022 5

First published 1968
by SCM Press Ltd
56 Bloomsbury Street London WC1

© SCM Press Ltd 1968

Printed in Great Britain by
Billing & Sons Limited
Guildford and London

MISSION IN INDUSTRIAL
FRANCE

CONTENTS

ACKNOWLEDGMENT

I SHOULD like to take this opportunity to express my deepest thanks to the SCM Press for offering me the possibility of sharing with others something of the ministry of 'La Mission Populaire Evangelique de France' to French secular industrial communities. To write this book would have been virtually an impossible venture but for the patience of the Editors of the SCM Press and the help in straightening out my English given by the Rev. J. T. Thompson and the Rev. W. H. Kyle. Mrs Willa Syratt typed the manuscript, and a final check was given by the Rev. Henry Roser, former General Secretary of the 'Mission Populaire', Dr Peggy Holmes of London University, and Bishop Russell White, Chairman of the British Committee of the Mission. I am most indebted and grateful to all these people, and equally so to all those others, agnostic and Christians alike, who have taught me and my wife to live as Christians in our French secular and industrial society.

GEORGES VELTEN

Le Foyer Fraternel
La Mission Populaire
Paris XIème

1

Meeting People

IT WAS the fourth time that François, a ten-year-old boy, had come to the Wolf Cub Pack meeting at the Mission Centre. In the courtyard and under the lime-tree in full blossom, the boys were standing in a circle; two of them, right hand stretched out, were taking the Cub's promise. François sighed deeply, and the Cub Leader could not help noticing that he was very upset. When the ceremonial was over he came over to the boy. 'What is wrong, François?', he asked. François raised his curly head, and answered sadly, 'I won't be able to be a cub . . .' 'Why not?', said the Leader. François looked him straight in the eyes, and said with another sigh, 'I cannot promise to be loyal to God. God does not exist.' Another boy laughed, 'Why bother? It's fun being a cub!' Soon after that François stopped coming.

Roger, a fitter in his early forties, had been coming regularly to group discussions on world affairs at the centre. One night he approached me and said, 'Do come and visit us at home.' The following Friday, I pushed open the gate of the little garden covered with flowers, and walked up to the three-roomed pre-fab where Roger, his wife and the three children lived. 'Let's stay in the kitchen,' said Roger's wife, 'it's less formal.' She put out a bottle of *vin ordinaire* on the table and two glasses, one for Roger and one for me.

The atmosphere was very friendly and, later on in the evening, Roger turned to the question of his beliefs. 'Let me tell you how and why I have become an agnostic,' he said. 'As a child, on my way home from school, I had to walk past the cemetery; in winter it was dark when we came out of school, and I was scared to death by stories about ghosts; I prayed hard, and I ran as quickly as I could! Now science has given me a proper explanation, and my children know very well that ghost stories are rubbish.' I made no comment. Roger went on, 'When my wife and I were a young married couple, and had to call the doctor to one of the children, we still prayed. But now we just rely on the doctor's medical knowledge, and follow his prescription carefully. Science heals. God is useless.' Roger sensed that I was not taking offence at his outspokenness, and he finished off by saying, 'You're well aware that I'm concerned about the welfare of the working-classes. In my experience, here again, God and the churches are useless. It's the working-class folks who will, in the end, manage to revolutionize society in order that all men should be respected.' Roger kept on coming to the centre, and eventually began to change some of his ideas, but he still maintains, 'The natural thing is to be an agnostic, and I still am one.' Some of the Christians at the centre, too, would say, 'The natural thing is to be an agnostic,' but they add, 'We have been convinced by Christ that he is alive, and have entered a personal fellowship with him.' They and Roger get on well together.

Paul had followed an opposite course to Roger. He had become a Christian as an adult. I remember calling on Paul and his family, during a strike which by then had already lasted over a week. They were living in another of those three-roomed pre-fabs, which they had furnished most attractively. One of their neighbours came in, and, after being offered the usual glass of wine, said, 'Brother, I have come tonight to ask if you would like a better paid job than the one you now have in the shipyards.' And he explained, 'A friend of mine is the foreman of a large garage in town, and wants a painter immediately. This job is yours if you want it, but you would have to take it now.' Evidently the visitor liked Paul and his family. Paul had been listening with an expressionless face, elbows on the table and gazing at a flower on the oil-cloth. He raised his eyes slowly and looked at his wife. They smiled at each other, and I could not help feeling how united they were. Then Paul startled me. He got up, and said very politely but firmly to his visitor, 'Sorry, brother, but I can't take the job. Don't you know that our department is on strike at the shipyards?' The man obviously knew. Paul's eyes flashed, 'Well, then . . .' But he didn't say anything but 'Goodnight!' The man got up, shrugged his shoulders, shook hands and walked out in silence.

After a minute or two, I was so baffled that I couldn't help remarking, 'As a minister, I just can't understand why you turned this man's offer down so flatly. . . .' Paul came round to me and said with a sad smile, 'M. Velten, you are still bourgeois.' I agreed that I was, but remarked, 'That doesn't explain anything.' Paul sat down, poured out glasses of wine for both of us, and said, '*A votre santé, Pasteur!*' He put his glass down, and went on in the tone of a good Sunday-school teacher trying to explain things to a rather stupid child: 'Didn't the Lord tell us to love our neighbours as ourselves? Who are my neighbours, if they aren't mates on strike with me? How could my wife and I dream of letting them down for the benefit of our own family, and still think that I could witness to Christ among them? It would be all up with me!' Paul gave me a few seconds to take this

9

in, and then went on spelling out every word as if he wanted me never to forget them, 'M. Velten, you are a minister, you are here to preach the Gospel, but not the Gospel wrapped up in a middle-class ethic!' I have always remembered what Paul told me on that night. Perhaps the help he gave me was the biggest I have ever been offered.

Edouard lived a good two miles out and cycled to and from the aircraft factory morning and afternoon, as many others did. His foreman had threatened to have him sacked for excessive drinking, and that is why he turned up recently at the centre to join the local branch of the Blue Cross Temperance Society. He had now been 'dry' for three months, and I was visiting him once again. He showed me round the house he had been redecorating. His wife was beaming with pleasure. I never imagined that our friendship was going to end a few minutes later. Edouard had promised to stop drinking 'with God's help', as the pledge-book of the Blue Cross puts it. He never went to church, but said he thought that he was a better Christian than many of those who did, and explained that 'the Church was not on the side of the workers'.

On that particular day I brought the conversation round to Jesus. 'What do you think of Jesus?', I asked. 'He was a good man,' came the answer, 'a friend to the ordinary folks.' I agreed and remarked, 'Isn't it a wonderful thing that he should be alive again, and that men should be able to enter into personal fellowship with him!' Edouard sat back amazed, 'What?! Don't you know that his life ended on a cross?' 'Yes I do,' I replied, 'but he rose from the dead!' 'Nonsense,' exclaimed Edouard, 'he did not! Nobody ever has!' It was my turn to be amazed; had not this man said that he was a Christian, didn't he think a lot of good of Jesus? I started to argue with him. But at that Edouard flew off the handle and shouted, 'M. Velten, are you trying to fool me? . . . or to fool yourself?' Edouard never came back to the Blue Cross. He told his wife, 'Velten wants to thrust his religion down my throat. I have not fallen so low that I have to put up with that!' It was a hard lesson for me to learn.

Crowded on the open space in front of the gates of the main shipyard, twelve thousand men or so had voted to stay out for a fourth week, 'until the boss is ready to resume negotiations about our wages, which are thirty per cent lower than in Paris'. The strike committee had another meeting, and a deputation called at the Mission Centre. 'This', one of the men said, 'is the one place in town where people who disagree can meet. Would the centre convene a meeting to see if it is possible to arrange to cook free meals for the families of the fifteen thousand workers on strike? And could we, please, have an answer by tonight?' We were sitting round a couple of tables pulled together in the tiny hall of the hut given as premises to the Branch of the Mission by the World Council of Churches. . . . One of the deputation explained: 'We thought that the group discussions on local or world affairs held in this place would form a good point of contact. The Strike Committee considers that there is a possibility here of getting everyone in town to support the strikers by providing meals for their families. On the other hand, there is the question whether it is the business of the Mission Centre to take sides in a strike? We think so, but we quite understand that you might like a few hours to consider the matter between yourselves.' Eventually we accepted the challenge, for biblical reasons, as I will explain at a later stage in this book.

In Paris, one fine February morning, several hundred thousands of people, at the general invitation of all the trade unions, did not go to work, or left work by 9 a.m., in order to follow the burial of eight people killed by members of the police during a demonstration for peace in Algeria. The funeral was to pass within two hundred yards of one of the centres, in the Avenue de la République. Some members decided to follow the burial, others to gather at the centre to pray. In Martine's office it seemed that nobody was walking out. Martine, a twenty-two-year-old typist, looked around a final time, got up and said, 'I am going to the Mission Centre to pray.' In a low voice, she went on, 'Yes, to pray for peace in Algeria,' and walked straight out.

That is how Martine became a laughing-stock among her colleagues until, after three weeks, she gave up and resigned her post. It took her a fortnight to find another job. What was wrong with these office workers? . . . or with Martine's way of witnessing? Martine said to me later on, 'Someone told me that I should have said what I did say differently, with secular words. It's difficult! But I'm not unhappy. I think I have suffered a little for the Lord's sake. Don't you, too, think that the Lord wants this war to end?'

It happened in Paris. Evelyne walked into my study, looking tired and sat down. 'I'm pregnant again,' she whispered. I visualized the small two-roomed flat with a kitchenette but no bathroom and no toilet, . . . and a family of four already. Evelyne went on, 'We've been on the waiting-list for a council flat for the last ten years. If we had a better house, I wouldn't mind having another child. . . . How is Jacques going to react when I tell him?' She took her breath and, looking me straight in the eyes, asked anxiously, 'M. Velten, would it be morally wrong for me to go and see an abortionist?' She added bitterly, 'Why aren't contraceptives allowed to be sold in this wretched country? . . . Why don't they build enough flats for ordinary folks?'

12

I knew perfectly well that in that year (1964) there were not going to be enough new flats built to house all those living more than six or seven in one room. . . . Birth control could hardly be the answer the Lord wanted to this problem, though I had heard some 'good' people advocating it on the grounds that it would not be as expensive as building flats for the half-million people living in Paris slums! Nor could abortion be the answer. . . . Then what? . . . What, for Evelyne and Jacques?

Pierre often comes to one of the centres. He is a retired journalist and a member of the Socialist Party. He has a beautiful white beard. He got up at the end of a meeting on 'The Origins of Man', and said, 'I respect Christians who are concerned with the welfare of the people, but one thing baffles me: why, to explain man, do you have to invent the hypothesis of God? I just don't understand it!'

2

A Look at History

AT LEAST 80% of French adults are agnostic and often firmly against the Church; this is markedly so in the working-classes. In Paris, for instance, 15% of the total population has some connection with a church, but the proportion of the working-classes connected with a church is a mere 1·7%. Children do not have religious instruction in school. While Roman Catholics are accepted as numbering between 10% and 15% of the French population, Protestants total only about 2%. Four hundred years ago, however, they numbered nearly half the French people.[1] It might be worth spending some time in considering how and why the present situation arose.

In August 1572, a large number of influential Protestants gathered in Paris for the wedding of Henri de Navarre, a Protestant and a cousin of the King, Charles IX. The Queen Mother, Catherine de Medici, a Catholic and, indeed, a niece of Pope Clement VII, who was in effect the real ruler of France at that time, took advantage of the gathering to further her own ends. She had for some time felt her position threatened, and attempted to re-establish her hold with a brutal massacre on St Bartholomew's day, the twenty-third of the month. Henri de Navarre was spared, but hundreds were assassinated in Paris and, as news spread, in the pro-

[1] In 1559, the date of the first National Synod of the French Reformed Church.

vinces. War started again between Catholics and Protestants. Henri survived the remainder of the reign of Charles IX and that of his brother Henri III, and after the assassination of the latter by a fanatical monk, he became King as Henry IV. A Protestant king was not acceptable to Paris, but Henri had a ready solution. *'Paris vaut bien une messe'* ('Paris is worth a mass'), he said, and became a Roman Catholic! He followed this compromise by giving freedom of worship to the Protestants under the 'Edict of Nantes'. This quite revolutionary Bill was signed by the King in 1598, and largely gave equal status to the two churches. On this occasion, the Vatican flags flew at half-mast.

Louis XIII, Henri's son, and his grandson, Louis XIV, nibbled away at this religious liberty, and in 1685 the 'Edict of Nantes' was abolished. Violent persecution by Louis XIV drove hundreds of thousands of Protestants out of the country. Others, not as many, went 'underground' and fled to the 'desert', to the south of the Massif Central. It took the best regiments many long years to overcome this 'rebellion'. Under these circumstances, thousands of Protestants became nominal Roman Catholics, to ease their position, while on the other side many Roman Catholics opposed the whole policy in disgust at the measures taken.

In the middle of the eighteenth century, under the influence of such philosophers as Voltaire and Rousseau, liberal and agnostic ideas took a strong hold in the minds of young people. Many came from homes which had given up the Reformed faith, or were dismayed by the religious action of the Roman Catholic Church. In the end, in 1776, the French Parliament passed the 'Edict of Tolerance', giving freedom of worship to non-Roman Catholics, but by that time there was only a tiny minority which had remained Protestant and faithful to the Reformation. Not long afterwards the French Revolution of 1789 removed the Monarchy and attempted

15

to break up the Roman Catholic Church. Napoleon, on the other hand, decided to revive Roman Catholicism to secure the stability of the State. He arranged for the Pope to be present at his coronation, but felt it inappropriate to receive the crown from the Pope's hands. Consequently, he himself placed it on his head! The Pope conceded Napoleon the right to appoint the bishops he wanted. Protestant churches were given a charter, but denied any form of national organization. Only people paying a heavy income tax were allowed to be members of the ruling bodies of local congregations.

During the first industrial revolution, which started in France at the beginning of the nineteenth century, Protestant churches were primarily concerned with missions at home and abroad, personal religion, and anti-Roman Catholic proselytizing. Protestants in towns and cities were usually middle- or upper-middle-class people. Without doubt, many approved of the 'Get rich!' doctrine of the Protestant Prime Minister of King Louis-Philippe; a handful held a more evangelical attitude. The Roman Catholic majority Church, too, favoured the wealthy and priests who identified with the workers, and the poor, the most notable of whom was Felicité Robert de Lamennais, one of the great revolutionary figures of the early nineteenth century, were either expelled or voluntarily left the Church.

Inevitably, it was predominantly in agnostic circles that the lower classes found champions to take their cause. The workers could only be un-churched – and anti-church.

This situation was sensed keenly by Robert McAll, the founder of the French Protestant Industrial Mission. In 1871, Prussian troops were in Versailles, the French Government had fled to Tours, two hundred miles from Paris, and the Parisians, the workers, were holding Paris against the

Germans. They had also overthrown their traditional bourgeois pattern of society, and the revolution of the Commune had brought to power the working-classes for the first time in French history, forty-seven years before the Russian revolution. The French Government signed an armistice with the Kaiser and ordered the French army to take over Paris. During the so-called 'Bloody Week', tens of thousands of workers were killed, tens of thousands were shot, tens of thousands were deported.

Hearing of this 'Bloody Week', a Congregational minister, Robert McAll, and his wife thought that they ought to spend their fortnight's holiday in Paris to see the French workers who had suffered so much during it. They took some leaflets in French stating who Christ was, and there they went, to the hottest spot of all, Belleville, talking in a friendly way to people, giving their leaflets out, and going into 'pubs'. Their French was scanty, but on one visit, a workman who could speak a little English stood forward and asked Mr McAll if he were a Christian minister. On receiving an affirmative answer, he said, 'Sir, I have something to tell you. Throughout this whole district, which contains tens of thousands of workmen, we cannot accept an imposed religion. But if anyone would come to teach us religion of another kind, a religion of freedom and reality, we are ready for it.'

The Holy Spirit worked on what this workman had said to the McAlls, and eventually, a few weeks later, Robert wrote to his deacons in Hadleigh: 'Having this summer visited Paris, we received a resistless impression of the urgent need for evangelizing effort there, and the readiness of many of the working-classes, through the influence of recent calamities, to respond to such efforts. Ability and willingness to undertake a charge like Hadleigh are possessed by many. Very few are so placed that it would be possible for them to give themselves to this purely mission

17

work in that vast foreign city. I trust that you will see that in taking this step I am actuated solely by a belief in a Divine indication.' I understand that one of his deacons called this a wild-goose chase.

On November 16th, 1871, McAll, his wife and her father left England for Paris. They had provided a little money by realizing their invested savings and by selling their few possessions – books, coins, some silver cups – which brought them about £100; a few friends subscribed some £25. They took a small flat in one of the worst parts of Paris, the Buttes Chaumont, and from there, in bitter weather, they reconnoitred on foot, wearily hunting among empty rooms and shops for a suitable 'locale'.

The one they eventually found was near the place of the original 'Macedonian Call'. It was opened in January 1872. 'Tonight at 7 p.m. a Free Reading Room will be opened, where pictures, magazines, etc., may be seen. During the evening, hymns will be sung and selected pieces read. English friends will give a warm welcome to everyone.' They had slipped hand-bills with this message under doors. Forty people were there that night. 'I would esteem', wrote McAll, 'forty so gathered as much as a thousand in England.'

In the following spring, Mrs McAll could write of the foundation of the Mission as a 'fait accompli'. Robert McAll had visited a number of Protestant ministers and laymen who, concerned as they were with the impact of the gospel on French people, volunteered to help him to start *'La Mission aux ouvriers de Paris'*, soon named by McAll, *'Mission Populaire Evangelique de France'*. For years and years, however, the Mission was known under his name, 'The McAll Mission'.

French Protestants responded so well to Robert McAll's appeal that within the next ten years a hundred, if not more, small centres were opened in a number of industrial communities. There might be a shop right on the pavement, chairs, a piano, a place where the story of Jesus of Nazareth and his power to bring new life into the present life of men could be told. But by then McAll was becoming convinced that he could not just speak about Jesus, that he had to help people to meet some of their needs. He therefore shifted the pattern from the small gospel hall to the settlement and community-centre pattern, where indeed, he pioneered in the field of welfare.[2] Unfortunately, however, from that stage on the churches ceased to be as interested as they were before. Was it that they were only concerned in having a pool out of which they could fish converts?

When McAll died in 1893, over seventy years old, the Mission was going through increasing difficulties because of a lack of financial support. If it had not been for the help coming from England, Scotland and the United States, the Mission would have had to stop operating. Nevertheless, individual ministers and laymen were still co-operating with the Mission, pioneering in the field of Christian action within the working-classes. During the Third Republic, towards the end of the century, State schools began. The first opened in 1885. They provided alternatives to Roman Catholic schools, and Protestant churches gave their schools and teachers to the State. Religious instruction was not allowed in the new schools, but children were given a day off, Thursday, each week for parents to send them to a church of their choice for religious education. This remains so in all primary schools. Religious education is optional in grammar schools; very few ask for it.

While working-class militants were in the main agnostic, the masses until World War II were nominally religious. This religion was mainly superstition, and so vague that

[2] The first welfare dispensaries, restaurants, libraries, holiday homes and, later on, scout groups, were started in the Mission.

with the influence of the present scientific and technical revolution there is development towards agnosticism. The majority of men, women and children have no knowledge of God through Christ, and to them everything seems to depend upon man. God appears to be unnecessary. For the 80% of French christened as infants, only 20% receive three sacraments,[3] and less than 10-15% retain an adult link with a local congregation.

Disestablishment of all churches took place in 1904, but in large circles of rural France and of the bourgeoisie in towns and cities, the Church remains part of 'the establishment'. The hierarchy of the Roman Catholic Church still controls several fields of the nation's life with considerable success. The Protestant Churches, with their very small minority of the population,[4] are made up of about 60% *Eglise Reformée* and 30% *Eglise Lutherienne*; most of the remainder are Baptists. Though small in number, the Protestants have given a number of outstanding civil servants of high rank to the State, and have many managers and executives in commerce and industry among their members.

The churches have never been part of the working-classes' 'establishment'. There has never been 'an indigenous church' similar to the Negro church of the southern States of America. The traditional churches are generally regarded as middle-class and bourgeois in life, style and worship, in social and political attitudes.

Before the nationalization of the mines in 1945, church pressures could be quite strong there. The presence of Roman Catholic schools built and supported by mine-owners meant that security of work depended upon children's attendance at the church school, rather than the village

[3] Three sacraments: Infant Baptism; Holy Communion (for the first and usually the last time by the age of nine or eleven; Marriage.

[4] See above, p. 14.

20

secular school. Some employers required a certificate of baptism before accepting a man or a woman. This practice is now almost extinct, though in some small firms a priest's recommendation is the best way to get a job.

It is understandable that French trade unions have little thought for the appointment of industrial chaplains. Immediately after World War II a number of priests concerned to bridge the gap between the Church and the working-classes had no thought of being appointed as chaplains. They accepted work as fitters, painters, boilermen, or in other similar occupations. When it became known they were priests, their workmates were cautious and suspicious, but eventually they were integrated into the working-class and were not only appreciated as workmates but were often elected as shop-stewards. Unfortunately, some Roman Catholic employers suspected that there had been a turn towards Marxism or Communism. The Pope, against the will of the majority of French Bishops, condemned the experiment. This action caused some working-class people to say, 'just as we thought, the Church is a reactionary organization siding with the wealthy'.

A positive interest in the French working-classes forces one to see and accept that they are segregated by history, and by the attitude of the rulers of the economy and the nation's life. They have become *a nation within the nation*. They have a highly subjective interpretation of their own past – events which to them appear as 'a glorious' part of French history would be construed by the bourgeois as tragic: for example, the revolution of the Commune in 1871. They have their own ethics, with a strong emphasis on collective ethics. They have a sense of the movement of history: like the Negroes in the southern States of America, they want to speed up the clock, whereas the middle classes wish to slow

21

it down, or stop it altogether. They hope for the emergence of a better society in the future, but the middle-classes, fearful lest they lose their privileged position, strive tenaciously to maintain the *status quo*, with the interesting and very important exception of technologists. These differences in attitudes to history and to individual and collective ethics are perhaps the most significant, but generation after generation of working-class people have also felt that they have not had a sufficient say in the pattern of society, nor the same opportunities of education, housing, income and leisure. If it were not for the collective pressure exerted upon private enterprise, Parliament and Government, they fear they could never hope to have the share of the national cake which is unquestionably their due. Middle-class people consider that it is their personal responsibility to improve their individual situation and criticize the working-class for their biased analysis of French society. Statistics, however, largely substantiate the working-class attitude, and the misunderstanding is just another example of the barrier between the classes.

Too often in the past the very few workers who did become Christians also became 'middle-class minded', which meant that they lost contact with their mates on the shop floor, and could not therefore communicate their Christian experience. Eventually their lives developed into two distinct compartments; they went to church on Sundays and worshipped God sincerely, undergoing tremendous and invaluable personal changes, but from Monday to Saturday nights they were regarded as foreigners speaking Chinese if they attempted to articulate their faith. So on the shop floor they felt frustrated and in the congregation they felt isolated. They could not whole-heartedly be middle-class Christians, so they were foreigners on both sides of the barrier. In the Mission Centres, and in a few industrial congregations in the

North, thanks to Robert McAll, Elie Gounelle, Henri Nick and others, it was possible for things to be different, as it was in one or two valleys of the Vosges Mountains in the Northeast, as a result of the work of Oberlin.

After World War II, a few Protestant ministers, a very few, also became worker parsons. The staff of *La Mission Populaire*, the French Industrial Mission, still has one or two. For such 'worker parsons' as for the 'worker priests', this has not been, and is not, just an experiment, but a new life in service of the Lord and of their fellow-workers. These ordained men have been the channels through which any churches which are prepared to listen have received and understood something of the real life and feelings of the working-class world. This genuine, but very limited, experience has probably been more successful in teaching the Church more about Christ than it has been in bringing the Church and the Gospel to the people in industry.

Even today, the main possibility for the organized churches to reach the working-class is through the life and service of the local industrial community. This is the method and emphasis followed now by 'La Mission de France', the Roman Catholic body that has superseded the 'Worker-priest Movement' and by ourselves, 'La Mission Populaire Evangelique'.

The workers of the Mission de France and ourselves could not but welcome the prophetic appeal to the churches issued by the 1963 Aix-en-Provence Assembly of the Protestant Federation. The hundred delegates, laymen and ministers in equal numbers, declared: 'We urge you to make the fellowship church manifest everywhere by uniting together in the service of all men. It is among men that the Church seeks the Living Christ, finds him and serves him. It is alongside men that we understand the love with which Christ loves us. It is in serving men that we receive the grace of unity among ourselves and with them. God loves the world, he gives to it his Son; he gives to it the Church, to proclaim the reconciliation with himself and express it in our lives. "They are to be one, so that the world may believe." He requires of you that you should be a Church for the world, and he will give you the power to become that Church."[5]

[5] I myself started working with the Mission in 1945, in the town of St Nazaire on the south-west coast of Brittany, a community of some 50,000 people engaged in ship-building. In 1960, I was moved to Paris and became Warden of a Community Centre in its east end. Through regular meetings and conferences, the staff of the Mission (about seventy people, including twenty-five or so ordained ministers) devised a common policy, and search the Gospel and industrial society to be true witnesses to God's love to our secular age.

Since 1958 I have been visiting Britain as part-time Secretary to the British Committee of the Mission, and this has enabled me to find out that the same concern, to relate the church to industry, is in the minds of a number of people there.

3

Christians without a Church

THERE has been a Protestant church in St Nazaire since 1885. The Eglise Reformée of Nantes, some forty miles away, built it for the few Protestant civil servants, teachers and shipbuilding managers in the town. Within a hundred yards of the church, since the early 'twenties, there has also stood a small community centre called 'La Fraternité'. This was not the result of the initiative of the Protestant middle-class people of Nantes or St Nazaire, but of the Nantes branch of the industrial mission, *La Mission Populaire*. In the early 'thirties, the warden of the centre was also put in charge of the church. Except for a few converted workers, the people of the centre did not go to the church, nor, with one or two exceptions, did the bourgeois churchgoers go to the centre. Each even held their own separate Christmas party, no matter what the warden wanted!

In March 1942, British troops landed and destroyed the main lock. The Germans could no longer make use of the port facilities to repair their largest warships. On February 16th, 1943, the US Air Forces bombed St Nazaire for the fiftieth and last time. There was nothing left worth destroying, and only 1500 people out of 45,000 still had a roof over their heads, not counting the Germans who lived like rats in their holes in the undamaged submarine bases until 'V Day', May 8th, 1945.

Nothing was left either of the church or of the centre. The

World Council of Churches gave a hut. It took the name 'La Fraternité' from the previous centre. One of the wardens lived in the hut, and the other one in a pre-fab, as did all those returning to their destroyed city. The centre had only one room, twenty-one feet by thirty, which could hold as many as 150 people, and a courtyard twenty yards wide and sixty yards long.

'Are we to rebuild a church and a centre with the government grant for war damages?' This is the question that people started to discuss by the late 'forties. The majority thought that all the money they had should go on a building useful for all categories of people in the local community, and that was definitely a centre, not a church. This was agreed, and the decision taken was considerably strengthened by one good lady, with a Protestant background, who had gone out of her way to advocate the necessity of a church 'for the Protestants to be able to count themselves and be on their own'. The National Committee of the Mission followed the local majority, and received the blessing of the central authorities of the Eglise Reformée. Local Protestants, therefore, have no church and run a community centre – the only one in St Nazaire for the benefit of the local community. At the time it made some impact on agnostic minds when the local press announced, 'the Protestants are giving up having a church in order to build a more beautiful centre for the use of everybody!'

It *is* a beautiful building, worth coming to St Nazaire to visit, as quite a number of people have done. The building has also set a pattern which a few Eglise Reformée and Lutheran churches are adopting on some new housing estates, giving a roof and a tool to a local congregation.

So, if you come to St Nazaire, do not ask for the Protestant church; people will tell you there is none. Ask for 'La

Fraternité', rue de l'Ile de France, three hundred yards from the railway station.

To get an idea of the aim and use of this building, you will not need to walk in. Like any other passer-by, you will only have to look at its ninety-foot frontage and its ten-foot-high mural, which you cannot but notice. On the right of the entrance door a large picture with four sentences explains the mural:

'At "La Fraternité", Christians and agnostics learn how to meet as brothers' (three men and one woman are discussing, and a dove is descending upon them);

'"La Fraternité" is concerned with peace and industry' (the dove – ships, cranes, workers unloading);

'"La Fraternité" is a place for parents and children' (a young couple with a little baby – children playing);

'"La Fraternité" opens the Bible in order that all men may be able to hear God's Word' (arms stretched out, a man shows a Bible to the people).

You might raise your eyebrows and think this a rather ambitious programme! But it might also be more than a programme: this book may perhaps show just what the Holy Spirit gives and enables Christians and agnostics to do together for the benefit of other people.

You are now at the top of the six steps leading to the entrance door. You do not need to come in to read, on a panel on your right, information about world or local affairs. Perhaps your own newspaper did not give you the Eglise Reformée's statement about the Bomb, or say anything about the number of people redundant in the shipbuilding industry? This is a place where you can become more knowledgeable about what is going on in the world of men. You sense it, without having to be told.

Without coming in, you can see how it looks inside. The door is a glass door, because these people live in a 'glasshouse'. The centre's monthly magazine goes out to most local people of any standing, and anyone can walk into 'La Fraternité' as easily as into a pub, at any time of the day. (French pubs are open from 7 a.m. to 10 p.m. with no closing hours, and have no curtains behind their glass doors!)

The place inside has formica tables surrounded by chairs. A great deal of light can enter from the front, which consists of large windows. The most important and interesting features of this room, which measures twenty feet by twenty-five, are three ceramic plaques situated at one end and set in a stone wall. The first one depicts thorns, nails and a hammer; the second, three people rowing in a boat, with a fourth at the helm; the third is a broken chain.

Anyone coming in for the first or the second time will ask the purpose and the meaning of these symbols. The answer is, 'To what do they direct your thoughts?' And so, as people should always feel free to do and really do in such a place, people start thinking and sharing their thoughts in an informal way.

Thorns, nails and a hammer have conveyed to most people that, 'there are thorns in the work in the shipyards'. An incredible number have said this, and very, very few have referred to Jesus' sufferings on the Cross.

The people rowing in a boat have not evoked the same unanimity: fishing in St Nazaire; people labouring together; these are coloured people, and we should not forget the underdeveloped countries; there are three Trade Union Congresses in France, and they should row together like these three for the sake of uniting the labour forces in the country; Jesus with his disciples on the sea of Galilee; Jesus teaching the congregation how to row together, etc.

In connection with the broken chain, everybody speaks

28

of liberation, most of the working-class world, quite a few of alcoholism, some of sin.

As we mention to people some suggestions which they have not given, the question which always crops up is: 'Which is the right explanation?'

Which is the right explanation? Few people, actually, have guessed before they are told. But it is as simple and as important as this: 'For you, the right one is the one which suggests itself to you! *You can go on coming here, and nobody is going to try to thrust down your throat things you do not wish to believe. But you are going to meet, here, people who are different from what you are yourself.*'

There is no proselytism going on in a branch of the Industrial Mission. But this does not mean that 'La Mission Populaire' would invite its workers to keep secret what they know of the Light and the Saviour of all men! This is a secret that has got to be shouted all over the industrial community, but not thrust into people's minds and hearts, in the proselytizing manner which people usually associate with Christians and Mission. To be a witness is not to be a 'saver of souls'. Only the Holy Spirit has the power to do this, not men, as these three ceramic blocks make perfectly clear to non-Christians and Christians alike.

On a Sunday morning, for the weekly service of worship, a slender and very beautiful wooden cross is hung on the stone wall in the middle of the three ceramic blocks. An open Bible is placed on the shelf which is set in the wall beneath the symbols. This visualizes the fact that Christ came into and still operates in this world of ours. The minister stands at the side. The people sit facing the wall, worshipping the One who was made man to carry all our burdens, liberate us from all evil powers and make us into a body of servants serving our fellow-men in partnership under him.

So the Lord is listened to, prayed to, and worshipped, and invites people to join in his Holy Supper in the very place where anyone can enter for any purpose connected with what the symbols and the mural in front refer to: the meeting of enemies, world peace, industry, families, listening to God who was made man – all matters with which the following chapters are going to deal.

The rest of the building is functional: a small and very nice theatre to seat 220 people, with a stage and a 16mm projector, a number of small rooms for children and youth or group activities, a kitchen for preparing communal meals, a front garden with flowers and sand for small children, a back courtyard for older children to play and for outdoor festivities. There are also flats for the two wardens, who are ordained ministers, as are the directors of all the branches of the Industrial Mission.

This is 'a church for others' in the mind of the passer by and not a building just for those who have 'religious needs'. Can a congregation be a 'church for others' if its premises are not designed accordingly? It is in the community that Jesus met people. Must not 'church premises' be community-centred?[1]

[1] The theme of the 1966 General Assembly of the Protestant Federation was 'Une église pour les autres'.

4

In Industry

THOSE who are looking for a thorough description of industrial France will not find it here. This chapter and the following one are concerned with the approach to industry and industrial society characteristic of the branches of 'La Mission Populaire'. It nevertheless seems necessary to give, in the first part of the chapter, a few general indications to help the reader to visualize part of the background of the world of industry in which the staff and the members of the industrial mission live and work.

France is not as industrialized as Britain. 28% of the active population (against 5% in Britain) are still engaged in farming. Only three conurbations number more than a million people, Paris with 7·5, and Marseilles and Lyons just over one million. The country is less densely populated than Britain, having only 120 people per square mile (against 200).

The industrial revolution started later in France than in Britain, at the beginning of the nineteenth century, and it was only by the end of the century that workers had the right to organize themselves in trade unions. Even today, from a legal point of view, the local branch of a union is nowhere officially recognized as having the right to be the spokesman of the men of the factory. There are few craft unions left, nearly all being industrial unions. Generally speaking, there is one branch for both skilled and unskilled labour of any one factory. The closed-shop system does not exist, with two practical exceptions, the Merchant Navy and the printing industry. This cannot be attributed simply to French individualism. If relatively few belong to unions, the main blame lies in the ideological split of the labour forces, with the result that France has three Trade Union Congresses, each factory usually having one branch of each of the three. The largest would probably be the CGT which has a communist or left-wing tendency. Next would come the CFTD, a Roman Catholic foundation attempting to become secular, and third, FO, with a right-wing socialist leaning.

In 1936 France had its first Labour Government, Le Front Populaire. Parliament gave franchise to shop stewards, two weeks' annual paid holiday, and a forty-hour week with the right to do overtime for extra pay. In 1938, the French Railways were the first private enterprise to be nationalized.

In 1945-46, after the Liberation and the first de Gaulle Government, further nationalization was decided upon: coal, some of the banks, electricity and gas. The National Health Service and the Family Allowance Scheme were organized. Every factory with a staff of more than fifty now had to have a Works' Committee, entitled to look into the way the firm was run and into the well-being of all those working for the company; but in practice these committees only operate as welfare organizations. An Economic (advisory) Council was appointed, with representatives of employers and big business, trade unions and family associations; the Council was required to make recommendations to Parliament on economic and social issues. The Government appointed a special agency to plan the expansion of the economy, and an advisory body. The largest TUC refused to sit on this advisory body, on the grounds of not wanting to appear to be sponsoring plans for expansion devised 'by private enterprise and government executives at their orders'. It is at any rate largely true that, since 1948, governments have not been 'on the side of the workers'.

The Expansion Plans, American subsidies and the Marshall Plan, the Coal and Steel Community and the Common Market have boosted the economy. But the Colonial Wars (Indo-China 1947-54, Algeria 1955-62), the decision to provide France with a so-called 'independent deterrent', and the government's 'stabilization plan', leading to deflation, have slowed down the economy. According to official statistics (1965), since 1958 and President de Gaulle's take-over, the income of labourers and semi-skilled workers has gone up by 5% (i.e. the same as the rise in the cost of living), the income of highly-skilled workers by 9%, and that of executives by 14% to 17%. The gap between people with a low income and others is therefore steadily widening.

It should also be said that the policy of the Gaullist régime has increasingly been to overlook trade unions and all representative bodies, and to embark upon new plans on its own and without consultation. The aims of the Fourth Expansion Plan, ending in 1965, have not been achieved in Education and Housing, though experts had thought them not ambitious enough. Less and less money is invested by the Government and private enterprise in fundamental research.

Automation is coming in slowly, mechanization is increasing rapidly. For example, the Peugeot car factories are employing two skilled workers to every one semi-skilled, but the proportion will be reversed within the next ten years. The company is also reducing the number of shop stewards and their power.

Other changes should come in rapidly: the school-leaving age of fourteen was to be raised to sixteen in 1967, and eighteen by 1970. The 1967 target has not, in fact, been achieved. Within the next twenty years agricultural production is to double, and the number of farmers to be halved. Less French coal is to be extracted, and more coal imported. Ten thousand supermarkets are to be opened, 60% more people are to enter the building trade, 50% more the transport trade, 70% optical industries, war industries, space research, information and television, 50% more the Health Service, 80% more schools.

There is a biblical necessity to welcome the industrial, technical and scientific revolution, as a gift of God to the potentialities of man.

Man has been created to dominate the earth, and here he is doing it (Genesis 1). He has been made a little inferior to God, and here he is showing it (Psalm 8). He has been given power to find out what normally remains hidden to man's eyes, and to go where no man has ever been before (Job 28). His little knowledge has been multiplied, and he can feed millions, house millions, heal millions.

If you had been at one of the Mission's training conferences for laymen in industry, you would have heard one of the staff, the Rev. Jacques Walter, saying:

'All human activity which aims at satisfying the real and imperative needs of men, as God's Word shows them, at releasing men from their state of bondage and at hastening their development, is a part of the scheme of salvation, for it leads to Christ. The community of mankind is, at one and the same time, the sphere in which God expects us to serve him, and the sphere in which he himself operates. This is why we can say that God responds to man's vital needs through the service of men themselves. We must reassess these needs according to the level attained by humanity and the stage of development reached by man today. Anyone who attempts to meet the imperative need of another man, according to God's Word, becomes that man's "neighbour"; and together they form the "cell" which is the basis of society. Christ is present in this social "cell", because he identifies himself with the man who is to be cared for. Unseen, Christ is there, in this "cell".

'Every man who opens his mind and his faith to this outlook on life is led by Christ. He is engaged on Christ's side in the battle for man. The work of Christ in this world leads to the development, on God's earth, of a world fit for man to live in, for man to regain his humanity and for society to become more human. Christ's intervention brings with it a profound modification of the structures of society. He leads us towards one goal – the Kingdom – and gets humanity to grow. By reason of the nature of his humanity, which crucified Christ, every stage of its growth confronts us with a new temptation – but it also calls us to a new deliverance and to fresh victory, because Christ rose from the dead. And every time, this victory is the recovery of our true humanity as it is shown in Christ, who is the true measure of man and society given by God himself. Christ is the prototype of the new humanity, and the prophet of the new earth and the new heaven that are to come. Nowadays, it is no part of the Church's work to direct the world. She serves Christ in the world, and seeks him there.'[1]

What does work mean for our people?

At one of our training conferences for laymen in industry,

[1] Before talking, Jacques Walter had read Matthew 25.31-46 aloud. After being for several years co-warden of Arcueil's centre (South Paris), Jacques Walter is director of the Lyons branch of 'La Mission Populaire'. This branch of the industrial mission was opened in 1963, on a new housing estate, at the request of the local Lutheran and Reformed Churches.

a nurse said, 'I am probably privileged. My work is perhaps more of a service. I am working directly for people.' Her statement caused a number of people to protest. 'We are all working for people,' they said, 'Why do strikes disturb so many folks if it is not because to work is to provide services to others?' And someone added, 'If it were not for the work of many, we would have no wine and no bread on the Lord's Table!'

It is primarily through his work, it was said, that a man serves his neighbours and participates in the upkeep of humanity. If the unskilled labourer very often has a feeling of frustration, it is because he has not developed his potentialities of service. But it is not on his own, but in partnership, that a man transforms matter and provides services for the benefit of others.

I well remember standing among thousands of shipyard workers at the launching of the liner *France*. She was their child. 'We made her,'[2] they said. 'Let's hope she will behave herself properly as she slides into her natural element.' And when she went, they walked down the shore and followed her as far as they could, with no heed for President de Gaulle, who was now giving his address!

In one of our conferences, a Paris Underground clerical worker, a communist who had become Christian, explained his attitude to work: 'I am always telling people around me that all of us must behave as members of one big family, from the bottom to the top. That is the phrase I use. It does not sound too political. It helps to put on the right track someone who is conducting himself with no care for others.'

[2] The power of man over matter is at the root of industrialization and at the root of a genuine and Christian understanding of work. But little has been written in French on this; the members of one of the Mission's training sessions were greatly helped in reading a lecture by John Robinson on 'Matter, Power and Liturgy' (*On Being the Church in the World*, SCM Press). See ch. 6 below, p. 69.

And he went on, 'It takes time and faith to be bothered with others. There is also always the risk of being criticized, for not minding your own business. But Jesus wants us to take the risk and be bothered with others: the people making use of the Underground, and those with whom we run the Underground.'

Nobody can serve the community without being in partnership with others. Therefore we must be seriously concerned with each other, and especially with those doing the 'dirty jobs', the badly paid, those who have a heavy responsibility, those who find it difficult to cope: the boy just come out of the craft school, the immigrants who do not speak French well.

André knows well and accepts that he has to be bothered with others. He is one of the shop stewards coming to one of the branches of the industrial mission, and a regular attendant at our training conferences. The other day, he approached the warden to have a word with him: 'The foreman did not like one of the men,' he said. 'This man had been in love with his daughter and he had put his foot down.' Eventually, the man got sick of being given what he considered were all the dirty jobs to do, and was very rude to the foreman. The foreman said, 'I am going to sack you if, within a week, you have not apologized.' The man did not want to apologize. What could André do to help? This is what he wanted to discuss with the warden and a few others.

Partners have more to do than just help one another. A coal-heaver told me, 'When a new man is hired, I always have a word with him and tell him, "The boss takes decisions which have an impact on several of us, if not all. So all of us must appoint a couple of people who will speak on our behalf. The boss is the spokesman of a group of people. We must have our own spokesman; and this is why I am asking you to join the Union and to take part in the branch meetings and to vote at the next election, to appoint the same or other suitable shop stewards. A body of people needs to have a steward, and the members of the body must consult to see what is the welfare and the well-being of the whole body." '

Relations today in industry are primarily collective. This is one of the results of the industrial revolution. It is also God's will that people should be members one of another: not only in congregational life, but at work. To want to get on by yourself as an individual is bad, in the light of the Holy Spirit.

In practice, the difficult thing for French workers is to choose which TUC branch to join, because of their different ideological bias. As one man told another, 'Your personal opinions can guide you, but the important thing is to bring within your branch a spirit of honesty and reconciliation with the other branches, not a spirit of competition, to get on with the responsibilities that all branches have to challenge together.'

One of the Paris evening papers was closing down. Jacques, a trade union organizer and a member of the Mission, was busy for a whole week getting printers to hire the lino-typists on the dole, and in the end he was successful. A few weeks before, he had been discussing the following issue at his Mission Centre: 'Printers are about to introduce new Linotype machines, on which they say they could perhaps put an ordinary shorthand typist. The Union has suggested that they should buy one of these machines and give time to the lino men to practise on them. They have turned the suggestion down.' Somebody listening said, 'Where could the Union borrow the money and buy one?', and this suggestion was eventually acted upon. Some time later Jacques said, 'It's a very strange feeling, at the age of forty, to start learning again. You give up a bit of your identity when you have to change your skill. . . .'

Highly mechanized industries, new machines doing more work in less time with fewer people, automation with its 'black boxes' – all are asking for quite a different approach from those engaged in production and distribution. In the end they will probably change man to some extent, as well as industry itself. How, nobody really knows yet. The participants at one of the Mission's training conferences thought they should seize every possible opportunity to put these three questions to people:

1 Who is going to have to pay for the suffering involved in the rapid changes in industrial techniques? Will it just be the ordinary workers?

2 Who is going to benefit from the growth of industrial power? Just a few, or all?

3 What is the ultimate aim of work and of industry?

One of the possible outcomes of mechanization and automation could be more leisure, and this, as a friend told me, would be 'very biblical', because the Bible actually says: 'Work must be followed, as a direct consequence, by leisure.' This friend went on, 'The National Committee of French Employers has officially stated that new patterns of work will not mean more leisure, for some time at any rate, so great is the need for manpower and so many are and will be the non-productive population, children and old people.' Nevertheless, this friend thought, 'We have got to be concerned in the Mission and in the Unions with more, many more, creative and educational possibilities for those who already have leisure to enjoy them.'

True enough! But everybody would agree in Mission Populaire circles and in union circles that for a very long time the life of people will primarily depend, for better or worse, on the way the economic life of the country is run. So it is no time for workers to give up their collective responsibility for shaping the pattern of tomorrow's industrial society. But I remember one Christian worker saying something even more fundamental. 'I don't think God will ever want us to separate our collective responsibility for serving our neighbour through our work and for shaping the pattern of work. The Church has more important matters to occupy its attention than merely to attempt to provide creative leisure for people, valuable though that may well be.'

Can the branches of 'La Mission Populaire act as 'go-betweens' in industry?

A member of the staff was once told by a friend of his and a 'worker priest', 'You have to make your mind up! If you want to be a witness to Christ among working-classes, you have to behave like a swimmer, crossing a river, who has stripped off all his clothes, because he knows he is going to land in a foreign country where he will have to start a new life and give up all his preconceived ideas and former ways of living.'

Broadly speaking, this is not the thing that missions have thought they had to do. More often consciously than unconsciously, they brought a civilization with the Gospel, not only schools and hospitals, but also a way of life. Today an increasing number of Christians realize that too often, outside the Western world and the middle-class milieux, we have no 'indigenous churches'.

When I myself started working with La Mission Populaire, a retiring minister told me: 'When a worker becomes a Christian, then his children, if not he himself, will climb the social ladder.' Like this minister, I then thought that this was a good thing. Eventually I was taught, by agnostics and a few genuine Christians, that an industrial mission had something very different to do than to help individual people to escape the ordinary fate of their mates.

To learn, I had to accept the role of someone who had to be taught. What I was taught turned out to be merely the Gospel of the servant.

'It is good to walk in Jesus' footsteps and remain a shop-steward, instead of accepting promotion and being appointed a foreman,' a boilerman told a coal-heaver at the centre. The boilerman was a Christian, and the coalman an agnostic who had asked what, if he were a Christian, he should be doing, accepting the manager's offer or turning it down. He replied, 'I had come to the same conclusion. I am happy that you concur from a Christian point of view. I can tell you that I will go on being interested in Christ.'

In quoting this conversation, my point is not that one should always refuse promotion. Nor am I inferring that a man could not 'serve his neighbour' when he has been put in a position of exercising authority over others.[3] I am, however, saying that Christ beyond question wants people to remain as the leaven in the loaf, as the salt in the ordinary broth, as the light in the darkest place. I am also asserting that, in France, when a man becomes a foreman he is *ipso facto* already 'on the side of the boss', as far as the man on the shop-floor is concerned. He has become part of the machinery which is speeding-up production, and imposing the standards fixed by management. He is part of a system which brings a tension, often a tremendous strife, between employers and employees, and he is on the side of management. Of course, we need to have good foremen! We need men of responsibility and courage who will, between themselves, stand shoulder to shoulder to play their difficult part as fairly as possible. Here is a challenge that Christians

[3] Foremen, supervisors and managerial staff are part of the industrial class, as trade union leaders now realize.

should not be afraid of undertaking. But there is also a Christian part to play, sharing the fate of the ordinary people. What witness will Christ have, what salt of the earth will there be among ordinary people if, when becoming Christians, sooner or later people come out of the ditch? Let's face it: in France, for a shop-steward to accept promotion is a 'counter-witness'.

In industrial France, workers and Christian workers are on one side, because they are workers. Christian leaders, whether laymen and workers, or ministers and members of the staff of the Mission, are not in the position of 'go-betweens', but in the position of men like Martin Luther King. In the South of the United States you belong either to one world, that of the Negro, or the other world, that of the white ruler. The Negro leader is not segregating people. They *are* segregated. People are what they are, and have limited possibilities according to the life they live and the fate that is theirs within a given group.

Why is it that Christian theologians and a very large number of church leaders have for many centuries realized and accepted differences between nations, acknowledging the importance of establishing the right and peaceful relations between these different national entities without denying to anybody the legitimate feelings of group-conscience; and why is it that such church leaders do not seem to want to accept that vital differences in industrial societies should also make people radically different, dividing them into opposed groups within one same nation, according to their place in the industrial set-up? Why is class-consciousness, especially among the working-classes, so often frowned upon?

Just as you would get laughed at, in the United States, if you said that there was no radical difference in the present fate and mentality of coloured and white people, so you would also get laughed at, in French industrial communities, if you stated that there is no radical difference between the working-class world and other classes. The bulk of the French working-classes *are* a nation within a nation, and regard themselves as such.

So we have no choice. We are on one side. And how could it be different, if the Christian witness is the collective responsibility of a group of men and women, headed by Christ and helped by a minister? How could laymen, i.e. working-class people, be in a position of 'go-betweens'? They are not.

It is only the individual minister who could pretend to such a position. In some parts of the world it might be possible, as I well know. It is not possible at present in France. We may well regret it, but we must be realistic and take things as they are.

Actually, the important question to be considered is this: if there is class warfare, how is the war going to be led? If one group in the nation wants to keep another group down, how are the 'underdogs' going to react, and how should they be induced to react?

Just as Martin Luther King knows that God's call, to him and to the Negro population as a whole, is to deal responsibly with their situation and meet the challenge, difficult as it is, with no hatred and no violence, but with collective non-violent techniques, so it is for us in France, with the same general perspectives, to act first for the sake of the under-privileged, and then for the transformation and the moral and spiritual benefit of those who tend, more often than not, to want to keep the 'status quo'.

Listen to this trade-union organizer, a Christian, speaking of his employer, who is also a Christian. 'There are two tables where I want to meet him. One is the table with a green cloth, in the board-room, for negotiations; and the other is our Lord's Table. I want to meet him at both, not just at one of the two. It is not just my own idea. It is the Lord's will, I am convinced. . . . And I know the Lord is waiting for us at both these tables.'

I would also like to quote one of my assistants in St Nazaire, a minister and a full-time trade union organizer of the CGT, addressing people at the centre. 'Our aim is not class warfare, but reconciliation. Reconciliation with justice, between "grown-ups" and not as between father and children. We want reconciliation, but not at the cost of justice.' And he illustrated what he was asserting, 'When I asked the General Manager of this company operating ferry-boats across the mouth of the river Loire for justice, I was asking first of all for the sake of his employees, the seamen, but also for his own sake, to increase his own human dignity, because in fulfilling my request he would face up to his responsibility *vis-à-vis* the owners of the company.'

Understandably enough, middle-class churchgoers and non-churchgoers find it difficult to understand working-class folk. They do not see the bar – not the colour-bar, but the class-bar – and only really mix with those belonging to their own milieux. They do not meet people of other classes face to face, not even in church, because churchgoers are generally middle-class. They do not intentionally look down on any social group, at any rate in church circles; and they would wish society to be good to everybody. They hope that things are not as bad as some people and some newspapers say; and usually they dislike the tone of these people and that press. They hope! They cling to their hopes, and too often become blind and deaf because they actually indulge in wishful thinking. But these people are nearly always good people, and now and then also God's people. So such working-class people, who have become Christians in the Mission

Centres, will have to, and actually do, *cross the gap* and come to meet these middle-class people for the sake of the unity of the Church and of mutual understanding in the world. It also equally happens that two, three or four middle-class friends may join each centre, to come and live their Christian faith with working-class people and meet with them the challenge they have to stand up to. It is rather like the time when whites joined with coloured in the march to Washington or in other cases; it is the Prince of Peace operating in his world and in his church. This service of the Lord has given the Mission the task of encountering people belonging to all milieux.

This must not cause us to forget for a minute that, this world being what it is, Good Friday happened before Easter. The Cross is the only way to the empty tomb, to victory over the forces of evil. We have first to set our hearts on Christ's Kingdom and his goodness, and so share in his sufferings and the sufferings of men, really to know why and by what power we sing whole-heartedly, 'Glory, Glory, Alleluia!' To have a few workers in a middle-class congregation might mean that this has happened, and the Lord should then be blessed with infinite praise. But many French church leaders are under no illusion, and acknowledge with real sadness that a few working-class people in the pews are a potentiality with as yet no visible significance.[4]

[4] *On having to take sides.* The Mission is far from being the only Christian organization called upon to be on 'one side', and its leaders have been well aware of the attempts made by others in a number of issues, economical and political. There were the authors of the Barmen Declaration who denounced Hitler's régime when the large majority of the German Christians and churches were not aware of its spiritual challenge. There was Karl Barth's attitude throughout the Second World War and the pronouncements of the Dutch ecclesiastical authorities during the same period. There were the statements made by the National Council of the French Reformed Church and the General Assembly of the French Protestant

How do the branches of 'La Mission Populaire' co-operate practically with those who challenge the fate of the working-class world?

Once a branch of the industrial mission is established in an industrial community, and suspicion from working-class people, trade union leaders, socialist or communist town councillors, etc,, is overcome; when personal relations are a reality for a number of people, and the centre gets known, it does happen that people of importance locally will call on the centre, as it is now looked upon as part of the industrial community. It might take a good five years to achieve this.

It will take longer when the city is large, and in such cities as Paris, Marseilles or Lyons it is sometimes practically impossible, as there is no borough life in large conurbations. Everybody seems lost in the masses. In that case, the training of individual men and women will still put them

---

Federation on the Atom Bomb (1951), Strikes and Economic Justice (1953), General de Gaulle's Takeover and Civic Responsibility (1958), the Algerian War (1960), the French Nuclear Deterrent (1963) and the Christian Faith and Nuclear Power (1967). Finally, there are the statements and declarations of the General Assemblies of the World Council of Churches.

Such statements seem to have been ignored most of the time by the ordinary minister and his congregation and not brought to the knowledge of the local secular leaders of the community. When taken notice of, they have been all too often criticized (or welcomed) on their political or class implications, and have introduced some of the tensions of the world within the local congregations. But it is their theological implications about the relation of the Church to the World and the World to the Church that are fundamental. When listened to, discussed and publicized primarily with reference to their theological implications, these statements have helped a good deal to foster a Christ-like corporate thinking and responsibility to society within, and often outside, the branches of the Mission, and within the branches of the Mission between people belonging to all levels of society. It should also be stated here that in three of its branches the Mission has also a possibility of serving management.

in a position to make some impact where they work, but, of course, they do not work where they live and where their Mission Centre belongs.

The majority of the branches of La Mission Populaire being in small or medium-sized industrial communities, it is worthwhile mentioning the part a centre and its members can play in a period of special crisis and also in day-to-day events.

It is the habit of French employers and central government local representatives to call in anti-riot police, called CRS, when workers go on strike and decide, for example, to march in a procession to the town hall to hand in a petition. The CRS (Compagnies Républicaines de Sécurité) are tough. They use sticks about three feet long, twirl them round and bang them on the heads of the demonstrators.

It is part of the techniques of collective non-violent action and part of the service of men that a warden of the centre should walk up with a trade union organizer to the CRS and say to an officer, 'We would like, sir, to be granted permission to proceed to the town hall.' The usual answer is, 'No! I have orders, and won't let the procession pass this point.' We reply, 'Will you please go and ask the commanding officer?' Usually the man feels compelled to go. We then come back to the crowd of several thousands and explain that we have asked permission to go to the town hall. It has happened that a police officer turns out to be helpful and even resists orders, given by radio, to charge the workers. If permission is not granted, we might try another route, or, addressing the demonstrators by loud-speaker, get them to go back home. When these riot-police start banging around, you never know who or how many are going to be injured. I have seen some men kept in hospital for several days. Even if fighting has started and workers hit back with anything they can get their hands on, trade union organizers and ministers have intervened to attempt to stop the fighting as soon as possible.

Happily the Holy Spirit gives you courage. You do not feel you have done anything by yourself. You have had to talk in a friendly manner to the police, hoping they will listen and not knock you on the head. You have explained, bluntly, but with patience, to the demonstrators that this march must be kept non-violent and that it is better not to answer the violence of the police by violence. It is difficult to stand up to this, as I well know through personal experience. But I may say that year after year in the community of St Nazaire I have seen more leaders and ordinary workers respond to this sort of approach to public demonstrations. The local council of the Mission has also asserted several times that to bring in riot-police, and quite often one CRS for every two workers, is no method of answering the workers' claim and their peaceful march.

The press does not always think it a minister's business to be with workers in a demonstration. For a certain section of the press, all workers are Reds, and the presence of a minister in a procession upsets their vision of the Church. It is pretty hard to put up with the insults of the press. But even if some are rather nasty, others keep your word, as the Lord said would happen.

If such events tend to be rather spectacular, they are happily exceptional. Personal contacts established in trade union circles, and the part played by a 'worker-parson' or a 'worker-priest' are more common, and in the long run usually more effective. For example, they might, as my assistant did, stand regularly in court as a union representative on behalf of workers frustrated in their rights. The influence of some Christians and agnostics, members of a branch of the Mission, on the way secular public statements are drafted is also important. Equally useful is the part a centre can play in helping sometimes militant union members with personal problems which hinder their service to their mates. It is again useful when a centre, at the request of the unions, organizes a street collection to find the money to send a deputation to Paris. It is important when a centre manages to get a number of people to co-operate in providing free meals for several weeks to the families of workers with no strike money (no French workers have this). Those private conversations where key-men suddenly decide to face the facts and sign a compromise with management, going against the will of thousands of workers sick of being humiliated, as too often they are, are also very important. It may be humiliation, but it is also learning that hatred is no definite answer, that the need is for negotiations conducted with steadfastness and the use of non-violent techniques. In no way less valuable are our regular training conferences for laymen in industry and all the informal conversations in the centres I have referred to, helping friends to stand up, as Christ's servants, to their day-to-day life in industry. But for each of them, a lot of their impact will depend on the sort of personal fellowship and spiritual discipline they achieve 'in Christ'. They are the only committed Christians among fifty or a hundred people! In an ordinary week, they may well never meet another committed Christian, whether Roman Catholic or Protestant, if they don't come to the centre. All of us need to stand on a rock!

St Paul had to be told three times, 'It is in your weakness that you will experience God's power.' And all of us on the staff of the Mission have experienced how unhappy it is to feel helpless so often! It takes time and effort to accept the fact of one's limited power and all one's weaknesses. When eventually you have, you perhaps pray a little better than you usually do. The Holy Spirit does not let you down, and so often does not let others, Christians or agnostics, give in to the inclinations of their lower nature. And through all the difficulties and sufferings, you do experience a sort of joy, a feeling that you are enjoying with others an extraordinary liberty that is indeed a gift of God. You also visualize that the whole of created life is straining and in travail, hoping for a new creation. Prompted by the Holy Spirit, you acknowledge that 'each time hatred and violence give way, each time justice and reconciliation come in, is definitely a visible sign that the Lord is at work and that the hope for a new creation is and will be fulfilled.'

5

Society and the Christian Hope

THE hope for 'a new earth and a new heaven'? This had played no part in my Christian life for years until, eventually, I was taught that ethics had to be based on a philosophy of history. Let me tell you how I discovered it.

'To hell with this filthy kitchen!' shouted 'La Chope', getting up and rubbing his hip. He was one of the thirty dockyard workers, all agnostics, who had volunteered to cook free meals for part of the families of 15,000 workers on strike. I was visiting the canteen. 'La Chope' hailed me and said, 'A friend of mine will pinch half a dozen steel brushes for us in the shipyards! We will have a beautifully clean kitchen, and no one will be in danger of breaking his neck!'

'I don't hold with pinching!' I said. At first they were all staggered, then 'La Chope', with a good sense of humour, said, 'Everybody does it, from the ship boy to the captain! And, anyway, tell me how I can go on working if I don't pinch a tool when my own tool has been pinched?'

This was greeted with a huge burst of laughter; I laughed, too, and then asked if I could make my point. 'Agreed!' was the friendly answer, which resulted, no doubt, from the fact that they knew that the Mission Centre was responsible for getting these free meals organized. So I asked, 'Do you think we are always going to have a world like this, one with sometimes the need to go on strike for weeks to get management to negotiate?'

This was a far-reaching question, but they were ready for it, and the answer came straight out, 'We won't! Society has to change, and will!'

I flashed back, 'I too, think it will,' and I added with a smile, 'Should pinching be going on then?'

They laughed, and said that it wasn't their wish that it should: it had more disadvantages than usefulness, they thought. I went on, saying, 'I hold the belief that this world will change radically through Christ, and Christ tells us that, if we really want a new world, we had better behave today as citizens of the world we would like.' They were clearly taking this in. I added, smiling again, 'This is why I think we should not pinch these steel brushes we so definitely need!'

After a minute or two the oldest man there, 'The Chef', as we called him, said, 'Agreed! I'm glad to know that you were not wishing to protect what might legally be the company's property, but morally is not.'

'Agreed!' said the others; and we decided to take the necessary money out of the canteen kitty.

This was ethics, moral principles, based on a philosophy of history, on 'eschatology'. But, believe me, I had not had time to prepare my answer! Most of the time we have to react immediately, hoping that the Holy Spirit will guide our minds and our tongues, as we have been promised by Christ. Next, we have to check back with the Bible, and see if the Spirit has had its way with us. This eventually leads us either to give glory to the Lord, or to repent and ask for his mercy upon us.

What do we mean by 'ethics based on a philosophy of history'? We mean getting events into perspective and deciding what is to be done according to one's understanding of history and specially of what lies ahead.

This is commonly done by people unhappy about the fate

of their nation or a part of the nation to which they belong. As we can easily observe in French industrial communities, such people behave like troops parachuted behind enemy lines preparing for tomorrow's new society to take over. This was also what the Resistance Movement did during World War II on the continent under Hitler's rule. Their moral principles and their whole behaviour were based on the certainty of the ultimate victory of the Allies.

Christians, sharing the unhappy fate of a nation or part of a nation, know that to die before V Day is to be given a divine and peaceful rest, which they indeed look forward to. But their main hope is still that the whole community will be rescued and given an entirely new way of life. This is the vision of the future that sustains them and gives them their moral principles. Abraham, like outstanding people in the Bible, thus had ethics based on a philosophy of history.[1]

For such Christians, as the history of the Jewish nation and the Church show, the spiritual danger lies in a possible confusion between their 'human' hopes and methods, and God's ultimate plans and will for the world. How could they know, if they do not refer to Christ's Word and his philosophy of history? Their sad fate prepares them to listen. There is a vital need for them to visualize the future of the world, and to have moral principles arising from their understanding of history. And this is so for the French working-classes.

On the other hand, any nation, or within one land, part of a nation, satisfied with the present state of their society, will not usually develop ethics based on a philosophy of history. Quite naturally such people do not see the necessity for society to move into a new pattern, but only the need to improve the present pattern. If they are Christians belonging to our affluent Western middle-classes, then understandably

[1] See Hebrews 11.8-10, 13-16.

enough their main hope will be their individual fate after their death. They will be rightly critical of such sects as Jehovah's Witnesses and all those who indulge in 'counting the days separating us from the second coming of the Lord' and who pretend to be 'cutting off relations with this perverse world'. But, not being driven to search for a philosophy of history, they might well read the Gospels without seeing the philosophy of history on which Christ's behaviour is based.

Eschatology is the name commonly given, among theologians and Bible scholars, to Christ's and the Holy Scriptures' philosophy of history. It is very simple:

Christ believes (and acts accordingly) that God's last word on humanity (*'eschatos'* means 'last' in Greek) is not the death of individual men and women followed by a peaceful and very welcome rest. God's last word will be the appearance of a new humanity, of which Christ himself is the prototype, a new humanity living in a new world into which he himself has been giving a certain insight by his deeds and his words. He affirms that those who believe in him during their life in the present world already share corporately in the life of the world to come, and as God's people (*laos*) have to give their fellow-men an insight into this world by loving them and walking in his footsteps. After their death, they will enjoy a needed and peaceful rest, and wait for the new world to open its gates.[2]

Ethics and moral principles based on Christ's philosophy of history are concerned with and entirely relevant to life in

[2] Suzanne de Diétrich in *Le Dessein de Dieu* and Oscar Cullmann in *Christ and Time* have well demonstrated that the Bible's philosophy of history has nothing in common with the Greek understanding of history and with the attitude of such people as Jehovah's Witnesses. According to the Scriptures, history is moving towards a goal and an end, the new creation, the reality of which can and must be experienced to some extent today.

industry and our industrial communities. I have said how I was led to discover it, visiting a canteen during a long strike. Behind the business of pinching or not pinching half a dozen steel brushes, there was, as readers and people there on that day were aware, an important issue.

In our industrial society, apparently, we have lost the Jewish and biblical understanding of private property, according to which the latter should be at the disposal of the needy (see Mark 2.23-28). The dockyard workers conceded that from a legal point of view these brushes were the company's property, but not from a moral point of view. This will seem debatable to those who do not know that management had kept salaries 30% lower than Paris standards, and that they were eventually to be raised 22% only after another strike. These dockyard men thought, quite naturally, that the company's property was the fruit of sheer robbery. Had I to take sides with the boss, and therefore give my blessing to the management's income policy? Had I, on the contrary, to side with the illegal attitude of 'robbing the robber', and therefore to imply that, from a biblical point of view, laws were unnecessary in the present pattern of society?

It seems to me, looking back, that only moral principles based on what the future will bring in (see Isaiah 65.17-25, especially vv. 21-22, and the whole Bible's doctrine of work) were able to give me and these friends the right attitude, that is to say to offer a fundamental challenge without adopting an illegal attitude. Christ is operating in this world. He wants laws as useful safeguards against evil-doers. He also wants people to behave according to the future God is planning and, therefore, gives others insight into these plans: people will not be robbed of the fruit of their labour and depend on earning money (see again Isaiah 55, etc.).

Of course, all the time we are walking on a knife-edge, and things are seldom clear-cut! If I may put it bluntly: things are never settled once and for all. But after all, have we not been warned that the path is narrow, that our doings are bound to be controversial, and that it is inevitable for us to have enemies within the world and within the Church? I have never liked it, and I hope I will never enjoy it! If I did, I would have forgotten that the only path to justice is to love one's enemies, and the only path to peace and service of justice. But in all this, there are two more points I want to make before drawing some conclusions. I shall try to do it by telling you the gist of the discussion, the informal Bible class, that helped us to make up our minds and decide to organize the free meals for the families of the 15,000 workers on strike.

One friend said, 'Look at the good Samaritan! He did not inquire whether the injured man was a decent person. Let's not start discussing the rights and wrongs of the people involved in this strike. The Samaritan took the risk that perhaps he, too, would be attacked, and spent some of his money to help. That is what we have got to do!'

'That is not the whole issue,' somebody else remarked. 'Is it the business of the Mission Centre to take sides in a strike?'

'Well,' said an agnostic present, 'if we don't get going in this centre, and if nothing is done for families with no strike money, we are on the side of the management. There is no neutral position!'

'Agreed! Neutrality is a catch,' flashed back a Christian. 'But listen to this; when Jesus multiplied the bread and the fishes, he gave people an insight into God's plans for the future world to come. If this place is seeking to follow Christ we have got to welcome the Strike Committee's suggestion and try to get people to organize free meals. It will be giving the local community an insight into God's scheme for the New World.'

'I am all for it!' said another Christian. 'But look, we are as poor as the disciples. Where are we going to get the money and the food?'

'Sorry,' interrupted another agnostic friend, 'the bulk of the people will not understand the motivations behind the centre's decision. They will say the centre is with the workers!'

Everybody looked at one another, and someone said, expressing more or less the general feeling, 'If you are right, and you probably are, we cannot do it.'

The Holy Spirit then used the first agnostic who had talked. This friend remarked, 'We all wish to be taken for what we are. But let me ask you this: was Jesus always taken for what he taught he was?'

I simply said: 'He was not.'

After a minute of silence, someone said slowly, 'Then we have got to take the risk of being misunderstood.'

The Holy Spirit was giving us 'the glorious liberty of the children of God' (Rom. 8.18).[3]

We looked at one another. Our decision was reached. We felt enthusiastic and full of apprehension at the same time. By the Lord's grace and the generosity he instilled in people, we did it. For example, in four weeks in the canteen I have mentioned we cooked and distributed 70,000 meals at the cost of 3d each. The Lord also opened doors for his Word to be heard by some. But others did not hear anything and sometimes closed their doors.

[3] A good twelve years after this happened, I read with great interest what Paul van Buren had to say about the 'secular' understanding of 'Christ is the Lord': his lordship being experienced as a possibility of putting events into perspective and freedom to challenge them (*The Secular Meaning of the Gospel*, SCM Press, pp. 140 ff.).

When I remember all this, my first impulse is to bless the Lord for his mercy towards us; and the Christian reader will probably want to do the same with me. But two points still have to be made:

How would we have got on without these two agnostic friends sitting in this discussion with us? I am convinced the Holy Spirit used them, as did Jesus the Samaritans and the Publicans, to show God's will to the churchgoers. Hence our conviction that *we have to listen to the Word with non-churchgoers to hear it fully.*

On the other hand, could any of us have reached any decision if we had not been a team of laymen *and* ministers? Could we, at a later stage, have achieved anything if our 'religious organization', the centre, had not been working with secular bodies? I am sure that we could not have.

Living in Christ, with ethics based on a philosophy of history, bridges the gap between Christians and agnostics, religious and secular bodies, and makes Christians become a corporate body with a vision and a responsibility, a body that eventually some agnostics are given the freedom to work with. For this to happen, it is essential that the Christians should provide themselves and the industrial society with an adequate organization, an adequate structure, and, if necessary, adequate premises for the service of all. In the French set-up a community centre can be a good tool. But, as in all social groups largely segregated within a national community, it is of importance for the Christian organization and its members to find ways and means of reaching those outside whose understanding and decision largely determine the fate and the future of the part of the nation they serve. How this can be achieved and is, in a limited way, being achieved, by '*La Mission Populaire*', I shall discuss in the Chapters 7 and 8 of this book.

Let us draw a few conclusions:

1 Our present scientific and industrial society cannot build by itself and with the materials provided by this world, a new society where no harm could ever be done. Justice, peace and brotherhood cannot be total, in spite of all the goodwill of man. To believe this is to indulge in wishful thinking. This world is, and remains, the world that crucified Jesus of Nazareth.

2 God is the architect and the builder of a new metropolis and a new humanity. We can see them in the distance, hail them as true and be quite convinced of their reality. They were made visible for present humanity in Christ and in the history of the Jewish nation, as recorded in the Holy Scriptures. Then people will not labour any more in vain. God will open the gates of this new world at a date that it is not proper for him to disclose to us. But things are ready. We must earnestly pray, 'May your name be honoured, may your kingdom come.'

3 Our present industrial society is not left to itself by God. Christ is at work in it. A vision of the new world to come enables us to appreciate what will one day definitely disappear and be raised to eternal life. It is in this world that Christ makes visible the world to come. We can therefore pray, 'May your will be done on earth as it is done in heaven', and make ourselves available corporately to Christ as his servants in the industrial society, knowing what has to die and what has to live.

4 Until the day God opens the gates of the new world, he wants this world to live. Each time men attempt to meet the imperative needs of others, they are engaged in the battle for man's sake on Christ's side and with him. We must pray, 'Give us this day the bread we need', and realize that God responds to men's vital needs by the service of men themselves. We must therefore make use of the present

scientific and technical revolution as a gift of God to heal, feed, house and educate all men living on earth. This is to be the ultimate and collective aim of industry.

5   We are no supermen, and our lower nature is a real problem. But let us not, in industry and elsewhere, bring up the subject of sin any sooner than we do when we pray according to Jesus' orders, not before witnessing to God's plan for a new world and to Christ's action to make visible this scheme and get men to meet the imperative needs of others. It will then be evident that man's lower nature is a real problem, and that human relations are therefore difficult between individuals as well as groups, classes, nations and groups of nations. We are always owing things to God and to one another, and are ourselves often misunderstood and judged with contempt. It is therefore indispensable that we should, in industrial relations and in relations between countries, forgive people, work for reconciliation and pray, 'Forgive us what we owe to you, as we have forgiven those who owe anything to us.'

6   If the new scientific and technical revolutions are giving us new opportunities to work with Christ, they bring along with them new temptations: seeking power for the sake of power, going in for wealth for the sake of enjoying privileges at the expense of others, etc. It is therefore of tremendous importance that we should earnestly pray, 'Keep us clear of temptation, deliver us from evil', and act, individually and collectively, according to the power and the goodness the Holy Spirit enables men to have.

It is the Church's responsibility to provide industry and the industrial society with groups of men and congregations having this vision and humbly asking for Christ's spirit to live up to it.[4]

[4] My references to the Lord's Prayer have followed J. B. Phillips' translation.

6

With Working-class Families

IT IS self-evident that while industry provides its people with an income, it is for the industrial community to provide such facilities as houses, schools, recreational opportunities, good transport to and from their work, and the structure for a community life. These are imperative needs which the individual worker cannot supply out of his own wages.

It is not enough, therefore, to criticize the present pattern of industry: we must also question the pattern of the industrial community. God always looks at man as a social entity.

In its concern for working-class families, an industrial mission is challenging both industry and the industrial society to which those families belong. Are the people's fundamental needs being met?

The industrial mission thus witnesses to God's concern for the whole of man (in a social sense) and presents to industry and industrial communities what should be their ultimate aim; namely, the fulfilment of basic human needs.

The average French worker has a family of three children. Since the opening of State primary schools in 1885, education has been free and compulsory, and, as we have seen, at present extends to the age of fourteen. The school-leaver may then try for an apprenticeship, but he cannot always find one. Few employers take apprentices. There are not enough craft and vocational schools. If things work out properly, by the age of seventeen he or she will pass a State Certificate examination and become a qualified worker and, by the age of eighteen, be required to do the work of an adult. When they reach the age of nineteen or twenty, all boys are called up for military service, which lasts for sixteen months. Male students will be granted a deferment, at the longest until they are twenty-five years of age. Only a minority of children have access to grammar schools, and no more than 3% of the student population have a working-class background. As long as young people find a job in the local community, they will stay with their parents until they get married. They will then set up a home of their own; but sometimes that does not happen until the first child is born. Only then do they really start paddling their own canoe, at about the age of twenty-four.

Can parents give their children a better education than they had themselves? Has the child an opportunity for religious instruction and going to church? Will he join a uniformed organization, go to a children's club or a youth club? Is he helped to learn what it will mean to him when he goes to work in industry? Does he get some guidance about sex and marriage from his parents or in schools? And what is the housing situation for ordinary families?

There is no religious instruction in State primary schools, and less than 15% of parents send their children to a church for that purpose.[1] Not more than 6% of the juvenile population (compared with 40-60% in Britain) join one form or

---

[1] Ethics, both individual and civic, are taught in school, but not religion. This was decided by the founders of French State schools in order to withdraw children from Roman Catholic influence. But schools remained closed on Thursdays for parents to be able to send their children to the church of their choice for the purpose of religious instruction (see above, p. 19).

another of organized activities for children or young people, and there is a great lack of open spaces, playgrounds, sports fields, and swimming pools. Though school leavers pass set tests in vocational centres, there are no 'From Learning to Earning' conferences organized by either education authorities, management or trade unions. There is no education about sex or marriage in school programmes; and a recent survey in Grenoble, a city of some 200,000 inhabitants, showed that over 80% of young mothers knew nothing about sex when they got married. The housing situation for ordinary families remains generally poor, especially in Paris; though there are some interesting exceptions, particularly in the provinces.

Is anything being done? Adult organizations, local authorities, the central government, Parliament, and the churches are becoming more concerned about children, young people, and ordinary families; and much more is being done than before World War II, especially where the majority on a borough council is communist or socialist. But when one takes into account the size of the present under-twenty age group and the natural increase in the urban population, under the Fourth Plan (1961-65) and the Fifth Plan (1966-70), public money has not been and is not being invested in Education and Housing to the same extent as was the case under the previous Plans and the Fourth Republic. Nearly all churches now run activities for the children of their own members (primarily uniformed organizations), but very rarely for the children and young people of the local community. However, thanks to schools' Parents' Associations, factory committees, and some churches, and despite the lack of support from central authorities, during the summer there are camps which provide one month's holiday each year, for as many as 1,350,000 children between the ages of eight and twelve, i.e. about one out of every five children of that age. This is by far the most important achievement since 1945.

What sort of a contribution is the Mission able to make here? The branches of the Mission operate in four particular fields: child-study help for parents; religious education; youth preparation for industrial life; and stimulation of local authorities.

There is a crying need *to support working-class parents in their task of bringing up their children.* Most working-men, Christian and non-Christian alike, are fathers. On the shop-floor they talk with one another about their families. The test of our support for these men is whether what they say is well-informed and constructive.

The twenty voluntary leaders of the Children's Club were having a final conference with Roger C., the director of the club and warden of the centre. They were going over a certain questionnaire, which they were to use as they went out, two by two, visiting the hundred families who sent their children to the club. The forms asked a number of questions:

Is your child keeping well? Has he been ill recently or had an operation? To what school does he go? What sort of marks does he get? What does he prefer doing at school? What are his favourite games at home and during the holidays? What sort of books does he like to read? How often does he go to the cinema, look at the television? Does he enjoy playing with others? How many friends has he? What does he like best at the centre? Does he tell you what he hears about Jesus? Would you like him to be a Christian later on? What sort of trade do you hope he may learn? For his birthday, or Christmas, what are you planning to give him? Does he get any pocket-money? Do you give him any guidance about sex?

64

'And please do not forget,' said Roger, the director of the club, 'to take these invitation cards for the Exhibition with you.'

Half of the leaders were young people of eighteen to twenty years of age, and half were mothers giving their Thursday afternoons to the club (no school, see above!). They all set out feeling rather nervous. Would not some parents treat them as intruders?

They came back delighted. Except for one occasion, they had been very warmly welcomed. Parents were moved by the interest being shown in their children, and a number said, 'This was the first time for months, if not years, that both of us have really taken time to talk about our children thoroughly. We feel we understand them better now.'

The invitation, which the leaders had taken with them, was to an Exhibition on 'How to buy books for your children'. A hundred and fifty parents came: two out of every three had responded. They went away armed with suggestions for books suited to the age and sex of their children. At the same time it had been a social occasion; people had enjoyed meeting one another, and many began to attend the centre or to call and discuss their children's behaviour.

A very large majority of parents do not go to church, nor do they want to send their children. It is therefore of the greatest importance that both parents and children should have *an opportunity to learn about the story of Jesus, without any obligation to link up with any particular denomination.*

At our centre in Roubaix, after various unsuccessful attempts to get fourteen- and fifteen-year-old boys and girls together, one day a notice was put up. Some people had thought the idea was foolish. 'From next Thursday onwards, after the Children's Club, from 6 to 7 p.m., there is to be a short period of reading the Bible together for all those over thirteen years of age.'

C

In the beginning, only four or five would turn up. Then numbers grew. Some had to leave promptly at 7 p.m. to be home in time for supper. The Bible readings had nothing formal about them. Participants laughed a lot. Not everybody listened all the time. Before we began, we drank coffee, and chatted about difficulties encountered at work or at school. Arguments would flare up. The Bible text was sometimes left far behind. Other questions were brought up: should we not organize a social evening? What shall we do next Sunday?

Nothing spectacular. Yet bit by bit they got to know the warden and his assistant, and found they had a place in the centre, whose aim some came to understand. This has been lasting for several years. Some entered into personal commitment to Jesus Christ. One was led to ask whether he could join the Blue Cross Temperance Society, to show his father, a chronic alcoholic, that it is possible to abstain from all alcoholic drinks. Another gave up part of his annual holiday to help with an Easter camp for children. Another, after joining the Army, wrote, 'I am engaged to be married. I am no longer keen to go overseas as I volunteered to do. But I know that my life is in the hands of One greater than I.' Written by that boy, those were not conventional sentiments. Two others came up shyly and said they wished to take part in the Lord's Supper. Some remained agnostics, but they had lived and discussed with others who had become Christians. They had caught some glimpse of Christian realities, and it has probably made a difference to their outlook on life.

Another task is *the preparation of young people to meet, as Christians, the conditions of industrial life*, through the provision of creative recreational activities.

In one of our centres in Paris, the members of the Youth

Club were invited to select from among themselves a team of boys and girls to compose a Christmas story. 'What sort of story?' they asked. 'Compose whatever you think suitable,' was the reply, 'a story that you can put on tape afterwards, and the Teenage Club will produce it as a shadow show.'

Some members of the Teenage Club drew the silhouettes, others cut them out and fitted them together, others fixed them on sticks, others built the shadow screen, and others arranged the electrical equipment. Everything was ready and rehearsed in good time before the Christmas Festival.

This was how the story ran: Marc, aged about ten, falls asleep on Christmas Eve and dreams he is going to Mars with an astronaut. He meets the inhabitants of Mars, talks to them about the earth and, with the help of his 'magic eye', a sort of telescope, shows them what is happening at Christmastide on earth in a number of countries. Afraid that his parents might start worrying a little, he asks the astronaut to take him back to earth . . . and wakes up on December 25th, with the pet cat still sleeping on his bed beside him.

What was the point of this project?

The truth was presented visually to both children and grown-ups, that the fact that God is Lord of the universe and Jesus is his true image is true for all the living beings there can possibly be, not only on the earth, but in all outer space. Would adult Christians and Bible class leaders have had the boldness of imagination to invent a Christmas story of such relevance to our age? Was it not better to rely on youth?

Moreover, the young people had to work very hard, evening after evening, with imagination and steadfastness, learning how to pronounce distinctly and how to control the tone of their voices. Last, but not least, they had to realize that each was only partly responsible for the success of the show, and yet, nevertheless, each must do his or her part with the utmost carefulness. The teenagers thus learned by experience that each boy and girl was merely a cog in the wheel, and yet that no cog is unimportant if the wheel is to perform its function properly and the show is to tick like a good clock for the pleasure and the information of all concerned.

Were they not thereby experiencing what it is like to work in industry? This was education for partnership in industrial work: but they were also being taught how to make the right psychological approach to corporate responsibility within a congregation! They were being helped to overcome their French individualism!

They were also finding out what degree of manual ability they had; and this leads us to consider the advantages of craft work, especially for children.

Craft work is one of the most commonly used educational methods in our children's clubs, for boys and girls from five to twelve years of age. They are offered a number of workrooms to choose from, irrespective of age or sex. Having freely selected whichever craft work they prefer, they are then obliged to stick to their choice: they will be expected to do their work well; they will learn to do it either on their own or in partnership with others: and they will give or sell their finished work for the benefit of the club. Thus all aspects of their craft work have an educational value and develop the following qualities: the responsible use of one's liberty to choose; steadfastness and application; awareness of man's power to transform matter; awareness that others have already worked to provide them with the materials they are using; the sense that one needs one's mates in beginning and completing one's own work; the vision of the usefulness of work, because it serves others by providing some of their needs or pleasures; the discovery that money is not something one will always be given, but something one will have to earn not only for oneself but for the group to which one belongs.

At the club, in craft work, the children find more than fun; they get a tremendous satisfaction out of it. It is all the more important, because, in our primary schools, they have little if any opportunity for it; and yet nearly all of them are going to be manual workers. It is obvious that a good deal of the educational value of each workshop will depend upon its voluntary leader, on his kindness to the children, on his understanding of their psychology, and on his ability to get them to discover informally the implications of their work and of their attitudes to it and to one another. The leader is not there primarily to teach them some manual skill, but to train them to become partners in an industrial society with the sort of spirit Christ wants all men to have.[2]

Clubs also provide children with other educational activities; outdoor and indoor games, stories, dancing, singing and drama. Programmes vary from one part of the year to another, and from one club to another.

The reality of Christ and the relevance of the Gospel are therefore made apparent both by the behaviour of the voluntary leader and by what the children themselves do in club activities. The leader cannot expound God's great design simply by telling the story of Jesus of Nazareth. He must enter into a certain type of human relationship with those he wants to see learning about Christ. Adults must break the barriers separating them from children by putting themselves at their service.

But it would be just as big a mistake not to tell the story of God's concern for mankind. Our children are not noticeably ready to listen to it. As one would expect, they share in the colossal religious indifference of the French workers.

[2] See p. 36 above.

When a child first hears somebody speaking about God or praying, he is utterly amazed and highly sceptical. Nevertheless, because God has been made man in Jesus, we are bound to speak of God by telling about the man Jesus. It is possible for any secular mind, child or adult, to become vitally interested in Jesus, so long as his words and his deeds are reported in secular language and parallels are drawn between his time and ours: between the Samaritan and today's non-churchgoers, between the lepers and maybe today's alcoholics, between the woman of Sychar exhausted by having to walk so far to draw water and present-day families having to share one tap between ten families, because they live on the one landing in the same Paris tenement. Then it becomes apparent to the agnostic child that Jesus is someone who puts human lives straight, giving back to people their human dignity, freeing them from the consequences of their sufferings or their misbehaviour, breaking barriers between social and religious groups. In fact, the child can see all this taking place in the club and the centre.

There are a number of methods which we use to supplement the telling of Jesus' story. The best, to us, are those where children are actively engaged in craft work, painting, drama, etc. And as a rule the leader will pray about matters which the children themselves have suggested. This not only makes them active and responsible; it invites them to enter personally into that secret relationship with the only One who has the power to convince them that Christ is his true image and that they can share with him day by day in his new life.

In addition, during the summer holidays, *a large number of children will go to one of the holiday camps of the Mission.*[3] To spend one or perhaps two months together will

[3] In 1967, 25,000 days of holiday camps were organized directly by the Mission's special branch 'Soleil et Santé' (Sun and Health).

add immeasurably to the educational value of the weekly afternoon or day at the club. Our children come from over-crowded districts and tenements. 45,000 to 50,000 people live in one-third of a square mile in the East End of Paris, with not a single open space where children can run about. One-third of the population are housed in tenements which allow only one room per family. For such children, a month in a summer holiday camp is no luxury. It is a necessity.

Some children are especially unfortunate. Practically all the families known to the centre in this East End district of Paris have had to send one of their children away to *an open-air school for several months*, on account of poor health. In such bad housing conditions, that is not surprising. It is therefore a privilege for the Mission that since 1945 we have been able to operate an open-air school of our own, in south-west France, at Arcachon-Le Moulleau, forty-five miles south of Bordeaux.

Other children are unfortunate in a different way. They are problem children, often because their parents have problems. Another baby may have been too much for a mother, living in one room in a tenement, and she has had a nervous breakdown. If the three oldest children can be taken from her for six months, she will recover and get on her feet again. Or again, the father may be away from home a great deal, because he is a long-distance driver, or perhaps he is in prison; and mother cannot cope with twelve-year-old Jules. Six months or a year in a children's home will make it possible for such children to come back and make a fresh start with the rest of the family. The branches of the Mission have long hoped for, and now possess, a long-stay children's home in one of the holiday camps, at Peyrebrune, where they have over seventy acres of open ground and woodlands, in one of the most beautiful parts of south-west France, La Dordogne, a hundred miles east of Bordeaux.

There is a need to stimulate local authorities and all other bodies who are in a position to care for children and young people and have a concern for the whole family life.

But to pull its weight in this field each branch of the Mission needs to possess adequate premises and to have the necessary resources to maintain them, to have qualified lay leaders provided with training planned especially to cater for men and women who have to spend eight hours a day at their daily work. What such leaders need, more than a knowledge of techniques, is a spirit of service leading them to give up a good deal of free time for the sake of others and a genuine interest in children and young people, so that they are able to love them with patience and firmness, no matter how tough they may be.

The branches of the Mission have to develop among their members a spirit of collective responsibility, dedicated service and fellowship, for the benefit of the ordinary child in the local community. One result may be that a number of the adult members of the branches will become active in the local school's Parents' Association. Such a secular organization is a good channel through which to bring pressure upon local authorities and central government agencies, urging that more attention be paid to young people in the provision of the facilities that only official bodies are in a financial position to give. A Parents' Association can put on its agenda educational activities for parents, and also be the place where those parents who belong to the centre can meet other parents who are equally concerned with the wellbeing of the children of the neighbourhood. A Parents' Association is also an organization where a newly appointed minister will learn what it is to be an ordinary citizen!

The future of an industrial community depends not only on the local prospects for industry, but also upon the opportunities offered to today's children and young people. Even if what the branches of the Mission are offering is no more than a drop of water in the ocean, they are giving a lead. They are also shielding young people from the danger of delinquency. The number of delinquents in France is surprisingly small, in spite of their inadequate environment. In new housing areas, where clubs are provided, delinquency is practically non-existent; for example, not one case has occurred, during a period of six years, in the district of Sarcelle, a new housing estate of 7,200 flats and some 42,000 people, twenty miles north of Paris. Let us not underestimate the potentialities of the industrial population!

What has been related so far has focused upon parents and children. But most branches of the Mission also care for those who are not part of the so-called 'active' population and therefore are not in so strong a position to place their needs before those who are responsible for their fate: old people, and the migrant worker and his family. Moslem North Africans are helped to learn to read and write, and members of the centres are inducing their trade union branches to stand up for the migrant labourer. But here again, as we see it in the Mission, our responsibility is not to tackle the whole issue by ourselves, but to give a lead and try to get other organizations and agencies, private and public, to face up to the issues collectively and responsibly, in the light of the Gospel.

Robert and Marie are an exceptional couple: active members of the Roman Catholic parish church, they are also active members of the local branch of the Mission. They first came to the Mission to read the Bible with Protestants. Their next step was to get involved with the senior minister in the 'Peace Movement'. The third step was to become one of those who helped migrant workers from North Africa to learn to read and write. Robert also found among his

Roman Catholic brothers a few people who were willing to come as voluntary teachers at the course organized by the Mission Centre. The number of pupils increased, and were soon too many for the limited space available on the Mission's premises; as a result, the Roman Catholic parish church is now running a course on its own premises, in co-operation with the Mission.

7

Two Diseases

YOU do not have to live very long in a French industrial community to come across people in trouble through excessive drinking. It does not take very long, either, to discover that abortions are commonly practised in order to control the birth-rate of a family.

How could 'La Mission Populaire' not be concerned with these two diseases? How could a Christian worker at his bench remain silent and inactive when he sees several of his mates injured because another man has been drinking to excess and has mishandled a machine or a heavy tool? How could a Christian neighbour remain inactive when he gets to know that the tension between a couple, living next door, is due to the fact that she has induced a miscarriage on herself for the third time and that her husband has been told that from now on he will have to give up making love to her?

Why remain silent and inactive when effective medical help can be secured, and when Christ gives us a lead and offers the power to put people on the right track?

First of all, we must look at the facts, and then see what Branches of the Mission have been able to undertake in these two fields.

It is well known that in France wine is the cheapest and the most usual drink. Nevertheless, the French are not wine 'addicts' in the sense that in Britain one might speak of drug 'addicts'. It is as natural to drink wine in France as it is to drink tea or coffee in Britain: but through lack of information, and in the absence of cheap soft drinks, 40% of the people consume more alcohol than the doctors advise. Half of them will eventually develop a condition of intoxication which will lead them, if not to alcoholism, at any rate to a position where they are less resistant to all forms of illness.

In factories, a great number of accidents are caused by excessive drinking, and on the roads, 57% of bad accidents are attributable to the same cause. Out of every ten men who drink regularly, only four live to be sixty-five, as against six out of ten among those who do not drink regularly. All French hospitals have a department dealing with alcoholics. In St Nazaire, with a population of 65,000, alcoholism cost the National Health Service about £700,000 in a period of one year (1960).

The other side of the picture is that some five million people make their living from the production and distribution of alcoholic beverages, i.e. one out of every eight or nine French people. But statistics are not enough to give a true picture!

At the end of a certain executive committee meeting, Eugene, the district secretary of the union, told Roland, a full-time trade union organizer and a minister, 'I want to have a word with you.' They went to the pub and had a beer, and Eugene said, 'Have you seen Pierre, drunk again? He is a good shop-steward, when he is not drunk, and a good member of the executive, when not drunk. But he is more often drunk than sober. Could you do anything for him at the "Blue Cross" branch of the Mission?'

Pierre is a very typical case: his personal problems interfere with his job. It is not uncommon among militants that a lack of restraint, in either their public or their private life, may affect their effectiveness and sometimes upset their whole outlook. The sheer necessities of a dedicated life puts a big nervous strain upon the stability of a couple and their family, and there is thus a danger that militants unconsciously should look for stimulants or tranquillizers. Alcoholic drinks are the easiest of all 'drugs' to take. They are the more dangerous, in that it is possible to indulge in excessive drinking without ever being drunk or aware that one is harming one's health, or even conscious that one is 'in need' of that extra drink.

To be effective, any therapy will have to take into account the private as well as the public life of the individual, his physical and his mental behaviour, and help him to rebuild his personality on the rock that is Christ. Like anybody else, he will have to accept his limitations, and find out that what sort of use he can be to others will depend upon what he really is himself. The Blue Cross Temperance Society's approach to a man is simply a continuation of the ministry of healing entrusted by Christ to the Church for society. The Blue Cross has given a lead to a number of people who are not especially preoccupied with alcoholism, but are concerned with the value of personal discipline and with the creation of collective support for the individual. Most branches of the Industrial Mission have a branch of the Blue Cross.

With Pierre the shop steward, as with others, it began simply with a signature which he was asked to give: in other words, he was treated as a reliable person in a matter where everybody, including himself, thought he was not the least bit reliable. He had previously tried several times to cut down on his drinking. He was now being asked to sign an undertaking that he would not touch alcohol in any form during the next twenty-four hours. He lasted out. From twenty-four hours to twenty-four hours, from twenty-four hours to three days, from week to week, this man and others re-educate their will. At weekly sessions they learn to understand their illness as much on the psychological side as in its psysiological and social aspects. Pierre was given a sponsor who was not, in his case, a former drunkard, but a member of the Blue Cross who had pledged himself to total abstinence and had learned to be a nurse. In private conversations, the sponsor helps the alcoholic to assimilate what he has listened to at the meetings, and to face boldly the heavy inheritance of the past. At the end of six months Pierre asked, as others do also, to become an 'active member', i.e. to do preventive work against alcoholism and to help others attempting to cure themselves. They thus complete the reconstruction of their own personalities, and discover a new sense of purpose for their lives precisely because of the defeat of their former existence. Eventually their standards may be higher than they would ever have been if it had not been for their defeat. It is good that this should happen in industry and in industrial communities.

The Blue Cross teaches that individual and group therapy must be inspired by the grace which is in Christ, and the alcoholic must avail himself of the power of the Lord. But how on earth, it may be asked, in French working-class districts which are almost entirely non-Christian, do you manage to show that God is behind all healing, and that Christ forgives and regenerates by his spirit?[1]

The means are simple, but no advantage is taken of a man's despair to do what he might call 'thrusting religion down my throat'. From the very start, he is asked to sign his pledge of total abstinence 'with God's help'. The words are printed on the book of counterfoils handed to him, but he is told at once that he can put these words in brackets. He is

[1] This question goes for all 'love' that the Lord is manifesting in any field of life.

warned that it does not mean that he is putting God between brackets, but that he is being given the chance to be honest towards God and towards his own conscience. Those who are Christian believers pray for him, and tell him they are doing so, as soon as they are sure that they will not offend him. He will usually take it well; in his own eyes it is a bit of a miracle that he can manage to 'keep off the drink', and another miracle is that he feels loved. He will also soon ask, 'Why do you tell me to stop accusing myself about my past behaviour? One has no right to wipe out one's past.' He will be answered, 'Regard your past life as dead, and yourself as free from the past. This is possible because of Christ. It is he who inspires our philosophy of life. Perhaps one day he will give you the experience of knowing that he is alive.' We leave our friend there, and leave his conversion to Christ, praying steadily that this man or this woman will let it happen – and it *does* happen. But even when it does not, we thank God that he or she has discovered a sense of dignity and a meaning and purpose in life. It is sad that only one out of ten lepers came back to give glory to Jesus, but Jesus healed the ten of them and did not run after the nine. Should we?

Anybody who has recovered from personal difficulties is called by Christ to put himself in a position of stewardship in secular society. That is why Blue Cross members are asked to give firm support to the preventive work of the local branch of the National Committee for Defence against Alcoholism, or to start such a branch where none already exists. In St Nazaire the Blue Cross gathered shop-stewards, trade union organizers and the general secretary of the shipyards into a Defence Committee. Within a couple of years, this is what they had achieved: in January 1959, 43,000 meals were served in the shipyard canteen, 42,000 with wine and only 1,000 with ordinary water. After introducing slot-machines which provided soft drinks into the workshops and beer and fruit-juice into the canteen, a year later, in February 1960, 44,000 meals were served, 23,000 with wine, 7,000 with beer, 5,000 with fruit-juice, and 9,000 with water.

This experience showed the possibility of inducing people to change their drinking habits, and how a works committee could play some positive part in influencing people for their own good. If there is, as we see it, no biblical reason for advocating 'teetotalism', there are undoubtedly biblical grounds for keeping not only spiritually but boldly fit (I Timothy 4.8). Another result of this experience was a noticeable decrease in the number of accidents in the works. This is just as much God's will for the security of individuals as for the output of the firm. Some people also became interested in the production of cheap soft drinks. Is it not God's will that men's products should be for the well-being of others?

Why, it may be asked, should a Blue Cross branch be included in a Mission Centre?

On the one hand, one of the dangers met in any local branch of the Blue Cross, as in any other very specialized group, is that of becoming a closed shop, a sectarian group, wanting to impose their way of life on others who are in no need of it, proud of what they themselves have achieved and are doing, satisfied with the sort of Christian faith they have discovered in their limited experience, and feeling no necessity to join a local congregation or to be concerned with the other issues which industry and industrial communities have to fight.

On the other hand, it is an advantage that Christians and non-Christians alike should benefit from the demonstration that people who appear to be 'lost sheep', can be made to become 'lights shining in the darkness' and 'salt', preventing a corrupted world from further decay. In industry and in industrial communities we need the demonstration that the deterioration of things and people can be halted. That is the very will and action of Christ.

More hidden and probably more disastrous is the other disease mentioned already, *abortion*. Statisticians have come to the conclusion that, year after year, there are more or less as many abortions as births: around one million.

Abortion became illegal with a Bill passed by Parliament in 1921, and is now a crime punished with imprisonment. Trials of abortionists are of frequent occurrence. One woman out of every two or three breaks the law at least once, with all the dangers involved from a physical and mental point of view. The large majority of women admitted to hospital for miscarriages have actually induced the miscarriage upon themselves, as doctors and nurses well know.

This is deplorable; but who is to blame for it? The blame lies primarily with the 1921 Bill, which also made illegal the sale of mechanical contraceptives and any publicity about contraceptive methods. In sex instruction in schools, teachers are supposed to talk 'only about mice', as an eighteen-year-old grammar school girl once put it. A teacher recently got into trouble with a Parents' Association for attempting to give sex education to her girl pupils. The subject is usually taboo between parents and their children. If one suggests to teenagers that they ask their parents what Mary's virginity meant, they will laugh and say, 'That would really put the wind up them! Please tell us about it yourself now.' It is also a fact that engaged couples seldom talk about the part which sex plays in married life, and that a married couple consulting a doctor about how not to have any more children are still all too often just told, 'Manage as best you can.'

It was in that rather hopeless situation that, in the middle 1950s, a lady doctor and a gynaecologist, a journalist, one or two other doctors, the National Council of the Eglise Reformée de France, and a number of ministers, took the bit between their teeth and founded a Family Planning Association. Doctors began to attend special courses. In a number of counties information bureaux were opened. The radio interviewed several people, including one of the staff of the Mission. There is now some hope that Parliament may allow the sale of mechanical contraceptives and the advertisement of contraceptive methods. If such a Bill were passed, it would make it all the more necessary for marriage guidance to be organized on a very large scale. Only extensive counselling and the availability of genuine contraceptive methods would effectively reduce the number of abortions, train people to responsible parenthood, and help them to experience love in the full biblical sense. But it must not have the adverse effect of furnishing local and central government with an excuse for reducing their housing schemes and their expenditure, in face of the imperative needs of ordinary people for adequate housing.

Most branches of the Mission have taken an active part in all these welcome developments. Ministers and laymen have learned how to talk about sex and marriage. The matter is brought up in all teenage and youth clubs, as well as with parents, who usually welcome this help and say, 'We do not know how to talk about these things with our children.'

Engaged couples coming to a centre for a religious benediction upon their marriage are generally told that this cannot be done unless they first come for half a dozen conversations about married life. One of the wardens, a layman or woman, will take charge of them. At first they frown at this demand, and say 'We still have so much to do before our wedding.' Their second reaction is practically always enthusiastic, and they express gratitude for the opportunity.

Women members of the centres have volunteered to be trained as hostesses for the Family Planning Association. Twice a week, for four or five hours, they will receive, one after the other, couples or just women, listen to their stories, see what they can say to help, and then direct them to a specialist (usually a gynaecologist or psychologist) who will be in a position to give them all the counsel and care they require.

A number of centres have offered their premises for an information bureau run under the auspices of the secular Family Planning Association. Before coming to such a decision, the Council of the centre has usually had to study all the implications thoroughly. Members of the Council have had to overcome in themselves the uneasiness which French people feel in speaking about a subject which is usually taboo. They have to be convinced that intercourse is, according to the Bible, first of all a way of bringing unity into a couple's life, and that the procreation of children is only its secondary purpose. They have to realize also that co-operation with a secular organization is legitimate, and that it is proper to give information to people without at the same time feeling obliged always to deliver the whole Gospel to them. They have to take the risk of providing information, even though some people may take advantage of it in a wrong way. Such difficulties are, after all, the daily bread of a Christian body of people involved in a secular society; they are never solved once for all but must be considered corporately in respect of each new issue.

Wardens of the Mission have been invited to lecture to several Ministers' Fraternals about marriage guidance. Hostesses and wardens have also spoken in Youth Hostels, Conferences, and Parents' Associations.

The whole question is being raised with Communists and

Socialists. The Communist Party has been very much against birth control on the grounds that Malthus, and many of his present-day disciples, advocate it as a method of reducing the birth-rate. Marxists are convinced that the earth can provide all that is necessary for everyone, if the economic pattern of society is really organized to meet the imperative needs of all. They believe that many want birth control as an alternative to the necessary changes in industrial and non-industrial societies. Without the Communist and Socialist votes, Parliament would not pass a new Bill, especially if the Roman Church does not come forward with a new approach to contraception.

Our members also discuss these matters with Roman Catholics.[2] The distinction which Roman Catholics still make between mechanical and so-called natural methods is, to our understanding, rooted in a misconception of the relation between science and faith, between mankind's new technical possibilities and the Church's outlook. God's power is not to be confined to the mysterious aspects of life which men do not yet understand. God has the power to teach man to act responsibly, in the light of the increasing knowledge that he is being given, as someone 'created a little lower than God' (Psalm 8, RV). Responsible parenthood is what we are asking Roman Catholics and Communists to teach to French people, and our wish is also that they should see that faith and science are not basically opposed to one another but necessarily complementary. This last point is of momentous importance for the Christian witness in our scientific and industrial age. It is when agnostic minds see that Christians are not opposed to the coming of age of man, that they may well start to take notice of the good news brought by Jesus of Nazareth.

[2] The Roman Catholics quite recently developed marriage guidance on a large scale.

We have learned in the Industrial Mission to greet with joy and awe the new potentialities of man. We have learned equally that individual and private matters have collective and political aspects, which are also to be considered under the light of the Gospel.

8

In Politics

THIS chapter will not be an attempt to describe the French political scene, which has changed greatly in the last twenty years, and will no doubt alter even more in the next two decades. Our concern here is with some aspects of the involvement of an industrial mission in politics.

It was a time in the early 1950s, during the Indo-China War. Etienne was on the dole. He walked in, 'Just to say hello', as he said. Eventually he disclosed what was on his mind. 'It's a problem at home just now,' he said, 'the little money you get on the dole!' I agreed; and he went on, 'It is monstrous to see so many of us, building workers, out of work, when practically two-thirds of St Nazaire is still waiting to be rebuilt. It was destroyed during the war by the US Air Force.[1] And there we are, destroying cities in Indo-China! The money spent in two days of this dirty war would get the building trade going again for a whole year in this city!'

Etienne sighed, remained silent for a moment, and then got up and started walking up and down the room, talking again in his deep voice. 'It made me angry the other day to hear that Social Democrat advocating that the Union should not interfere in politics. We've got to get this war stopped, if we want to get things going again over here!' He sat down

[1] See p. 25 above.

to recover his breath, and added apologetically, 'We must also stop it for the sake of the people over there. Why not stop it at once? In the end we shall just have to give in.'

I poured Etienne another cup of coffee. I was very disturbed myself about our hopeless economic and social situation in the early 1950s, not only because the building workers were out of work, but because of all the families who were having to live in the country, outside the town on the farms, with only one room each and no sanitation, being forced to travel in to work by train or bicycle over anything up to twenty miles a day.

Etienne went on, 'As you know very well, I am an agnostic. Pardon me if I ask you this question: some people say that religion has nothing to do with politics. And I have always agreed. Now I see the Mission Centre interfering on the side of the poor and the oppressed, and I am wondering whether you will get into trouble with your Protestant authorities for working for peace in Indo-China?' He sipped his coffee, and with a wink and a smile, asked me, 'Aren't you being as left-wing as I am?'

Etienne immediately saw that he had embarrassed me. My answer was blunt. 'If someone tries to follow Christ, do you think he needs to belong to the Left to be against this war?' It was Etienne's turn to be embarrassed. He replied, 'I have told you I am an agnostic. I don't know a thing about Christ. I don't understand what you mean by "following Christ". To me, if you become active in politics, it can only mean that you must have political motivations. We were taught in school that it was missionaries who helped to colonize the overseas countries, and that government money has continually been given to the mission schools and hospitals. Why didn't the missionaries let people believe what they wanted? All religions are equal, and the important thing is to be sincere.'

Etienne apparently began to feel that I was not taking in what he was saying. He got up, with a sad smile. 'I am sorry, friend,' he said. 'We are not on the same wave-length, even if we agree that this war should be stopped without delay.' He went on, 'It is time for me to get home, just in case my wife wants me to give a hand with the children. Must try to make myself useful. When are you holding another meeting in the pub about Indo-China? I'll try to bring some of my neighbours along.' And off he went.

Actually, while listening to Etienne, I had been thinking. 'This man is quite typical of a number of French workers. A good father, a good member of his union, a good citizen with a good political conscience. An agnostic and a man who sees that everything is tied up with everything else. He realizes that it is nonsense to try to departmentalize the daily life of the man in the street into politics or economics or religion. The whole lot is bound up together.' I was also praying to the Lord, thanking him for Etienne's wholeness and frankness, and that such a conversation had been possible. But I also confessed my unhappiness that it is so difficult for agnostics to understand that we Christians get our impulses from the One we believe to be the real Prince of Peace, who one day will melt all weapons into ploughshares and build a new world of peace and justice.

It is our belief in God's scheme for the future, and our confidence in the present power of the Lord of all lords, which compels us of the Mission to involve ourselves freely in issues where the imperative needs of men may be and often are jeopardized. We are obliged to acknowledge that a number of issues of a political nature must be challenged, and that there is therefore an evangelical necessity for some sort of political action to be devised.

As a result, we try to become knowledgeable about political organizations and political events. We take time to read, and time to get to know leaders in the industrial community. Lay leaders and ministers have to be as well informed and as much in touch with key people as any member of a political party, and must understand the relevance of the Gospel to the political field.

Our centres become places where the 'wolf' and the 'lamb' learn how to meet one another on a friendly footing: the Mission is not known as an organization identified with one political faction, but as a place where people who disagree fundamentally with one another can nevertheless genuinely meet. One of our lay leaders once said, 'Only one thing can get men and women closer to one another, and that is for them to discuss together what they disagree about.' The local branch of the Mission does not hesitate to call key-people and ordinary folk to meet on controversial issues, such as the future of the industrial community, or a referendum, or some aspect of the international situation.

At such encounters people develop a way of speaking which, whilst it is critical, will not hurt the feelings of others. They learn to express their own motives without trying to thrust them down the throats of others, and without waving the flag for their own organization. Such meetings call for someone in the chair who has authority, patience and vision; it may not be the warden, for he may well not have those gifts.

Each branch has one or more teams of laymen who feel responsible for keeping contact with various political organizations sometimes by serving in them. The warden does not necessarily hold back, but it would be wrong if he were the only liaison officer. In order to serve, some men and women of the Mission become able to help the political organizations to formulate their policies and to choose the best ways of carrying them out. They know how to employ lectures and meetings, deputations, the writing of statements and petitions, and at times take a hand in the organizing of demonstrations. There are difficulties and risks. One's motive for participation may be misunderstood; one may get knocked about by the riot-police. But it will be found to be a good opportunity for developing fellowship and mutual understanding, especially if a leader from the centre is able to serve by taking the chair in committee meetings. And there may be chances of inviting people to respond to Christ's call to seek reconciliation and goodness and to pull their weight for the benefit of others.

In these ways, several people in each branch discover the relevance of the Bible's philosophy of history and of Christ's word to a number of present-day issues. They will be equipped to play an active part in their trade unions as well as in the community. Yet many of those same people will at first have feared that they would never be able to exercise any civic responsibility except that of putting a voting paper into the ballot-box!

A further result has been that a number of leaders of the industrial community, some Christians, others agnostics, have got into the way of meeting their opposite numbers from other secular or religious bodies; and they have found themselves undertaking certain enterprises together along non-violent lines. Sometimes it has become possible for them, in appropriate circumstances, to publish agreed statements – for example, about Germany, or about Algeria, or about world peace.

In this fashion, the centre becomes part of the life of the industrial city and of several of its leaders. Good personal relations are established. Most doors are open to the leaders of the centre. Secular organizations reckon with the Mission. Reconciliation transforms tensions into fruitful polarities.

The idea of attempting such forms of service as these, in an industrial environment, usually makes one feel one's insignificance. But it is surprising what the Holy Spirit enables ordinary people to achieve. There is no substitute for personal prayer and self-discipline minute by minute, if one is to expect that one's attitude will be welcomed as a gift from him who so loved the world that he gave his Son for it. One must believe that he still gives to industrial society those who are his Son's body.

How easy it is to speak about prayer in this context! But how difficult it is to practise prayer, both in the fire of action and in one's quiet thinking about the problem of involving the Mission in politics. Our prayer is not to avoid, but to face conflict, whatever difficulties may ensue.

For instance, can the warden of a centre just decide on his own that he will go speaking in pubs about Vietnam or any other issue, without the Council of the centre first having the opportunity to approve his action? What if the minister thinks he is compelled to such action, but the Council disagrees, on the ground that, willy nilly, in the minds of local people, he also involves the centre just because he is the warden? Even if the permanent staff and the Council see eye to eye on the question, is there still not the danger that any who may not agree with them will be inclined to stop coming to the centre?

Again, can a little group of Christians count for anything in large secular organizations like political parties or trade unions? Aren't the Christians going to end up at least as mere 'fellow-travellers', if not as the helpless prisoners of such bodies? Or will they enjoy 'the freedom of the sons of God', and really 'shine like lights in this dark world'?

It is hard for people, who are in the main agnostics, to imagine that guidance can be given to Christians from a non-visible power at work in this visible world. It is very difficult for them to see the connection between 'divine inspiration' and the story of Jesus of Nazareth whose life, in their view, ended on a cross. Several will argue that it is impossible for them to give credence to a so-called 'divine' inspiration, or to evangelical and non-political motivations, when they see that the national churches do not all have the same agreed attitude to an international issue; or when they see local churches not backing up and implementing political utterances made by their ecclesiastical authorities. The lack of unity in the Church about secular issues is a stumbling block for the agnostics. We have to face it. However, whilst admitting our weakness and disobedience, we should not be without hope. The Holy Spirit is leading the Church to a new awareness of its responsibility to the world. We ourselves have valued and generally found helpful the statements made by national and international Christian bodies.

When the World Council of Churches, or the French Protestant authorities, do speak publicly about God's will in secular issues, another big difficulty is that the press usually does not mention it, nor do local church magazines appear always to have the space available to publish it. How, then, can people be informed? Each Mission centre takes such statements seriously, publicizing them to those who come to the centre, and circulating them to all town councillors, trade union organizers, local MPs, and as many other responsible people as possible.

All this can only happen if the leaders of a Mission branch do not regard neutrality as the way to secure unity within the centre. Only obedience and love, with suffering and long-suffering, can create Christian unity. Leaders of a branch have to be utterly convinced of this.

Our conviction is that we must not let ourselves be paralysed by the very real difficulties of the Christian witness in politics. There is, of course, the need to be wise, and first and foremost the necessity to seek God's inspiration through his Word with the utmost energy. The Council of the branch is also careful not to commit all its members, who retain the right to differ. The Council can only publish a statement, or decide upon a policy, on its own behalf, as a body of people who accept a certain collective responsibility for leadership. According to the Scriptures, there is a place within a congregation for such a group of people who will humbly act as 'prophets', undertaking the responsibility of articulating publicly God's word in a given situation.

Nevertheless, however wise and bold we may be, we receive our share of criticism, and are now and then libelled in a rather nasty way. But there is also a number of people who will listen to our words. The important thing is to make it clear that our motivation fundamentally is a love for people. This is, of course, far from easy to achieve. But we must not have any feeling, or convey any hint, of hatred towards those who misrepresent what we say or do; never speak ironically of people who are responsible for a policy we feel compelled to attack; and never despise those whose actions we have to denounce. These are attitudes which cannot be maintained simply by relying on human nature and its impulses. These are the fruits which the Holy Spirit manages to produce in us ordinary people, both in Christian circles and also, thank God, in agnostic circles.

It is equally vital for men and women of the Mission, when they become Christians, to bring their whole concern for the present world into their weekly corporate service of worship. It has to be part of their corporate worship, if their worship is to be according to God's will, and their service to the community to be genuine. It is usually not left to the minister alone, but becomes the responsibility of all those who sit 'in the pews', to decide upon the subjects of the congregation's prayer on behalf of the world. We try not to act without corporate prayer. If we are led to pray about political issues, we need to listen to God's word about politics. Then should the sermon deal with politics? Definitely! But not as though the minister were the Prime Minister addressing the House. Nor should it be a humanitarian address, dealing with what the preacher feels to be the lowest common denominator of the interests of the people in the pews. We are careful not to indulge in such false attitudes. What is possible and enlightening, we feel, is to recall how the Jewish prophets took sides, and to compare the facts and the people they challenged with the present-day issues we have to deal with. Or, we listen to the comforting assurances which Christ gives us that he is not leaving this world to the powers of destruction which would bring us to total chaos. But because during the sermon our worshippers can only remain in the role of listeners, we often prefer not to preach a sermon, but after a shorter service on a Sunday morning confine a political subject to a brief address, which is then followed by informal discussion. Alternatively, we take up such matters in a weekly meeting, or in small gatherings in private homes. We believe that it is necessary to provide opportunity for discussion about controversial issues, if we are to find out what light God's word throws upon them. By talking together people become better informed, they digest what they hear, they learn how to articulate, and eventually how to bring up such issues either with their mates on the shop-floor or with their neighbours. They will know how to react to those who say that they find politics difficult to understand and so have chosen to leave the subject to the so-called experts and to the government.

An industrial mission can also help the institutional congregations – indeed it has a special responsibility to do so – to witness to the concern of the Lord for the total life of men and nations. The Mission now and then speaks to the Churches, interpreting to congregations in industrial neighbourhoods the feelings and reactions of the working-class world and awakening the Christian conscience to problems of peace and justice. Thus industrial mission and institutional denominations are then involved together in the Christian witness about political issues.

9

The Mission and the Church

'LA MISSION POPULAIRE', like any other industrial mission, owes its existence to a few Christians who are concerned with living the good news of the Gospel in industry and industrial communities. But those few Christians are members of the Church. It is the Church which they want to relate to this 'alien' world. They want the Church to be present among those who are foreigners to her. Therefore they seek the Church's understanding, her concern, her prayers, and her support in men, money and policy-making.

Does the Mission get more than the crumbs left over, once all the traditional machinery of the Church has been provided for? This question, so often asked, is ultimately not a good question, because it implies that an industrial mission should be at the receiving end in its relationship with the Church. In reality, *the Mission is at the giving end*. It provides the Church with much more than it takes from the Church. That does not mean that an industrial mission gives the Church something to boast about, as a mother might be proud of what her children have achieved. It is to the Lord that glory should always be given, as we all well know, when some valuable Christian work is performed. What we are utterly convinced about, in 'La Mission Populaire', is that our centres are just doing what an ordinary congregation should be doing, and that our work provides ordinary congregations with laboratories of Christian experience, where serious research is carried out into what it means to be Christ's body in a local industrial community. We are not aiming at providing the Church with one more institution. We are being the Church in industry and in industrial communities. It is a simple matter of being at the disposal of Christ, who is already at work there. Is this not what each traditional congregation is called to be and do, and what an increasing number are becoming more and more concerned about?

The reader may well object to the assertion that our centres are laboratories for the benefit of the ordinary congregation. Admittedly this book has not yet dealt with conversions and the life of the congregation. But our centres do have congregations. They are born out of service to the community, and their life is to serve the community. They do not exist apart from that service, nor can they exist before people enter into active obedience to Christ. They are born in the midst of secular society and during the process of serving it. They do not have to go 'into the world'. They are born there, where they live and work, in the midst of a suffering nation, amid the continual changes of urban and industrial society. It was necessary in this book first to record the process of involvement and service out of which those congregations are born. Now follows a description of the new type of congregation which the Mission is adding to the Church, and the sort of relationships established by such congregations with the traditional churches.

For people in a local industrial community, an established centre is a place into which they walk nearly as easily as into a pub or a supermarket or a cinema, and they leave it just as freely. If they come back regularly, they soon find out that, without having to commit themselves religiously, they can easily enter into personal relations with a number of people

D

and enjoy their fellowship. They next discover that a number of 'regulars' are not there just for their own sakes but for the sake of others. So many different things are going on that a number of helpers are needed, and, to their surprise, they may volunteer to do one thing or another without having to show any particular religious interest. For example, if a branch gives an annual Christmas supper to six hundred 'down-and-outs', or tries to collect £400 in the neighbourhood for the poorest old folks; if meals are to be provided for thousands of workers on strike, or hundreds of posters are to be stuck on walls around the neighbourhood about the international situation; if a monthly magazine has to be printed at the centre and taken out to six hundred or a thousand families, or if a youth festival is organized; there is plenty to do. And so the newcomers start coming for the sake of others.

This is how you find yourself involved in the work undertaken by a Christian congregation and sharing in the work, without having had to become a Christian. At this stage you no doubt know that some have become Christians here, that the Bible is opened and studied in this place, and that services are held on a Sunday morning or a Sunday night. Mere curiosity, or perhaps a genuine interest after some particular conversation, may get you to come to a meeting especially concerned with the direct understanding of Christ. You may, however, never do so, and yet still feel, and be looked upon as, a full member of the centre, just as much as those who have become Christians. They have joined the congregation: you have not. You will know the difference. They believe that Christ has risen, and that they are in fellowship with him. They say that they have not come to this conclusion by themselves, but have been convinced by his Spirit. They look upon themselves as his partners, with the corporate responsibility of being at his disposal for the service of local people. They read the Bible, they pray, they worship, they celebrate Holy Communion, they make a serious offering of part of their earnings. They believe in a divine reality. You do not: but you get on well with them, and you will do a number of things with them as an equal partner – things which need to be done for the benefit of industry and the local community.

People tend to be quite outspoken about their position in relation to Christ. There is Pierre, a member of the Blue Cross, who has been mentioned already. Up to now he has remained an agnostic. He tells newcomers how to sign the undertaking 'with God's help'. 'It's up to you,' he usually explains, 'but remember, please, the organization believes in that help. Personally, I would not have given up the drink without the help of the Blue Cross, but I am not yet convinced that God is behind it. Some have become convinced. Have a word with So-and-So. He will tell you more about God's help.'

Then there is Henry, who eventually became a Christian. Like Pierre, he belongs to the Communist Party. For him, at first, it was a stumbling block to hear that Jesus is risen. But when he was told that it is only Jesus himself who can convince a man that this is true, his reaction was, 'If Jesus, and not myself, is to bring me to this belief, I won't worry, and I do hope that it will happen.' Six months later it did. His agnostic friends were staggered at first, and wondered anxiously, 'Would this lead him to give up being a militant?' In the long run they thought it had improved him.

Why this difference between Pierre and Henry? We do not know, and should we enquire? The only thing to say is that Henry did 'ask', 'seek' and 'knock'. Why did Pierre not do the same? We have decided to leave that question alone, to remain his friends, as we always have been, and to pray, not forgetting to thank God for what, through Pierre, he is already doing for others and for ourselves. Pierre has helped us, just as Samaritans helped practising Jews who followed Jesus in the midst of the nation. Pierre has also benefited from God's love because Christians have become his neighbours, first through the Blue Cross and then in other ways. But I cannot forget why Pierre said that he would go on being interested in Christ: on that evening, he had come up to the centre straight from the factory, and he told a group of us: 'I have been offered the job of foreman. I'm curious to learn from you what a shop-steward like myself would be doing in this particular case if he were a Christian.' A boilermaker, George, was prompt to reply to Pierre: 'We badly need foremen who like the man on the shop floor; but a foreman is on the side of the boss, and Jesus said that he came to serve and that we are to walk in his footsteps. As a Christian, I think I would have to remain a shop-steward.' 'Thank you,' said Pierre, 'that is the way I felt. Any other answer would have been a blow to me. You have confirmed me in this new opinion of mine that Jesus has something to say to all men.'

The cases of Pierre and Henry show that it is vitally and spiritually essential for a congregation to live in such premises, and with such a spirit, that fellowship can grow up between Christians and non-Christians who are all equally preoccupied with serving industry and the local community together. The building used should be adequate to be a sort of community centre; that is important. What is more important is that Christians should be corporately concerned with imperative human needs, breaking down barriers between people, and with them trying to listen to the good news of the Gospel. For this to happen, Christians live 'in partnership' in Christ, day after day becoming a body of men and women of whom he is the head, 'for the benefit of the world and for God's glory'.

For a number of reasons, in 'La Mission Populaire', as in other industrial missions, we were very reluctant for a long while to recognize that one necessary result of our work would have to be the birth of congregations. It is possible that we were made cautious because of the existence of a number of local churches which had become frozen and inward-looking institutions. But we were led to discover several years ago that, according to the Scriptures, the Christian belief of individuals must lead them to become a responsible corporate body of people, with Christ as their head – in other words, a church, even if that church will have to be of a new pattern.

In 'La Mission Populaire', therefore, the time is now over when the converted were passed on to the neighbouring Protestant church, Reformed, Lutheran or Baptist. With the churches' consent, the new Christians stay in the centre and gain experience there of all that it means to be 'in Christ'.

There is no being and living 'in Christ' if there is no listening together to Christ's Word, no corporate sharing of his supper, no collective worshipping of God, no communal renewal of individuals through mutual forgiveness, absolution and sanctification. There is no sharing in Christ's life and work if there is no common prayer for a corporate ministry to the world, and no fellowship of prayer with other churches.

When a new branch of the Mission opens, the 'church' may well comprise only the two or three permanent staff and one or two other people. From the very beginning, this little group will be the church, ministering along with agnostics of goodwill living in the neighbourhood. Year after year, the Lord adds members to his local body. It is usually a long and slow process. After ten or fifteen years they may number fifteen, thirty, sixty, sometimes a hundred people, or even perhaps one hundred and fifty: no bigger than the leaven in the 'lump'. But God can achieve big things with a small nucleus, and he does. Days may come again, as they did long after the apostles' time, when people will crowd into the church once more. We do not see why this should not eventually happen. But it is no use day-dreaming about it. The only way to hasten such a day, if it is to come, is to face the present secular age and do our best to be faithful.

Despite the colossal indifference of our fellow citizens, we are given the full presence of Christ himself day by day, and Christ gives to the things made by man the power to reveal God's scheme for the world. Ordinary bread and ordinary wine are made by Christ to point to the gift he made of his life, to his present undertakings, and to what he will still achieve. The fruits of man's labour, by the action of the Holy Spirit, witness to and make visible Christ's words and deeds, past and present, as well as the new world and the new humanity to come. And the few people who gather together for this meal can say, as a friend of mine once said, 'It is wonderful! We are just like the ordinary bread and wine on this table. When we let Christ have his way with us, what we are and what we do in industry and in the community points to God's scheme and God's love. I find in the Lord's Supper the pattern of what he is doing with us from Monday to Friday.'

It is a great joy to celebrate this visible sign of God's love. Most branches observe it on the first Sunday of every month and again on Christmas Day, Easter and Whit Sunday. People stand in a circle facing one another round the table, and sometimes the circle has to squeeze itself into the aisle between the chairs. Before going back to their seats, people will look up at one another and sing together a hymn of praise, sometimes hand in hand, or shaking hands at the end of the hymn. Responding to Christ's invitation thus becomes not just an individual act, but a visible entrance into a fellowship. It is also a commitment and an offering. In most branches people come up to the table and leave an envelope with their monthly offering. For numbers of them it means 10% of their earnings, as is suggested in the Bible. That 10% is only a suggestion which is put to them. Envelopes remain anonymous. To live on 10% less than one's earnings is possible, if one remembers that many people earn 10% less than one does oneself, and if one is first of all convinced that this is the Lord's requirement for our lives and the fruit of our work to be his.

From one branch of the Mission to another, with the general consent of the churches, variations are introduced into the Holy Communion service. The loaf of bread will remain on the table; the small pieces of bread are kept large enough for people to realize that it is bread which is given to them, because Christ is the Bread of the world; one or two common cups and the plates for the bread may be 'secular' vessels, as a reminder that things are not holy in themselves but that Christ gives a spiritual value to plain and ordinary things. This is why St Paul could write to his correspondents, 'You are holy.' We are helped to remember that sanctification is a process that must be started all over again every morning of the week. Are we not all ordinary folks, prisoners as all men are of their 'lower nature', but loved and brought to life and obedience day after day? What help is it to us, in our understanding of the way the Spirit works with those who belong to God, if the buildings and vessels and all else the church possesses are once for all declared 'holy'? Do not people need to be led to realize that the majority of things in our secular world can be made to signify God's purpose and love?

Another important feature of our services is that people become visibly active. Not only do they walk up to the Lord's table, but any committed Christian knows that he may be asked to distribute the elements. In several branches, it may be the congregation and not the minister who decide the subjects of the intercessory prayers which come at the end of the service. This makes the minister a steward of the abilities of his congregation: he helps his members to be responsible for their corporate prayers.

To illustrate this matter, let us take one of the Paris centres. Before the service, the people used to hold a prayer meeting, 'so that we could pray for what we ourselves thought suitable', as someone explained. This meeting was not well attended, and at one monthly Council meeting, somebody suggested that, 'since it is the Sunday service which brings the congregation together, that is the proper time and place to hold the prayer meeting'.

This suggestion drew no serious objections from the laity, and no one asked 'Is it not the minister's job to decide for whom and for what we pray during the prayer of intercession?' They were not being disrespectful. They behaved as people who had reached spiritual adulthood. What they did argue about were the practical difficulties: 'Some will talk too much, and others will not open their mouths.' A Bible-class leader suggested that, 'The minister should do what I do with the children: come down from the pulpit and ask us for our suggestions'. Several retorted, 'We are not children. It would not work. The shy ones won't utter a word.' Eventually, one member of the Council made a practical suggestion, which everybody agreed to try out for a few Sundays. By general consent it has been going on ever since.

In this particular branch, the first part of the service follows the Liturgy of the Eglise Reformée: invocation and hymn of praise; Scripture reading, reminding the congregation of God's will for all mankind, followed by a response sung by the people; general confession of sins and a sung response; absolution and a sung response; confession of faith and a sung response. Then come several minutes of 'Quaker silence'. Along with their hymn books and the Order of Service, the fifty or so people present have been provided with a sheet of paper, and 20-30% of them will write down one or more subjects for prayer during the period of silence. The minister ends the silence with a word of praise: then someone gets up, collects the papers and hands them to him. The service goes on with the reading of the Word, a hymn and a short sermon, two or three minutes of silent worship, another hymn, the offertory and the dedication; then comes news of people and what is going on in the centre, for a full five minutes or more; after that, everyone bows for the prayers of intercession. The minister has had time during the silent worship following the sermon to spread the papers on the pulpit and look at them, crossing out subjects that overlap. Now he reads out the subjects and prays with the congregation in the ordinary secular language in which they are worded. The service ends with the blessing and a sung response. It has taken just an hour.

People will stay on for another half-hour or so, to meet one another. On the first Sunday of the month, the service starts with the Holy Communion, is followed by the 'Quaker silence', and then goes on as on an ordinary Sunday. Once every six weeks or two months there is only the first, liturgical, part of the service, which will last about twenty minutes; then people either divide up into small groups for a Bible study, or stay together. In the latter event, the minister or somebody else briefly introduces a general discussion on a topic which members have requested and which is related to the life of industry or the local community and to the witness of the centre. Here again people become corporately active, and work out what they think and what they ought to believe and do. People need more than to pray together about matters relevant to their daily experience;

105

they also need to think together, and therefore to talk together, so that they become articulate Christians from Monday to Friday.

For a minister, it makes a world of difference to serve such a congregation. He is learning from his people all the time: he is being taught how to pray in the language of the plain man; and he is being told the issues which the laity has to face. He is not pulling the people along, but helping them to decide corporately where they want to go, according to their own understanding of God's will. He ceases to be the 'specialist' who knows all about what it means to be a Christian 'in the world', and he becomes the Bible scholar who helps people to allow God to shed his light upon their affairs and upon their fellow-men. It is all very demanding for ministers who have been trained in French theological colleges: but what is very helpful in the branches of the Mission is that working-class militants are outspoken and not ready to accept the minister's word just because he is the minister. It is very enlightening for him to go back to the Scriptures and study, for example, Ephesians 4.10-11. He will realize that it is the local corporate body of men and women who are called to continue Christ's ministry. It is his people who are to be Christ's body in the local community, to proclaim God's word on specific issues, to announce the good news of God's scheme for the world, to take care of individuals and institutions, to heal the victims of diseases, and to mediate between God and people. Ministers are there to help the congregation to carry out its ministry, not to perform Christ's ministry by themselves, with the laity's help.

Though this may sound pure theology, it has become a living reality in our branches. For example, one day the members of the Council of one of them told the minister that they were unhappy about the way in which he conducted the monthly meeting: they wanted to revise the way in which the meeting was organized. They therefore wished to appoint a special Commission on which it was hoped that he would not serve. He was given the inward grace not to feel hurt by their suggestion. He understood later on that his friends had felt robbed of their collective responsibility for the leadership of the branch. A month later, the Commission came back with suggestions which the Council approved.

The outcome is that nowadays a layman introduces the meeting with a short Scripture reading and a prayer. The minister sits still in the chair. For the next twenty minutes or so, in a couple of sentences each, the twenty members, if they so wish (and usually they do) report on what they are happy or worried about in their own personal affairs, in their life at work and in their responsibilities in the centre or in secular organizations. When this was first suggested, the minister remarked, 'Are we not here to deal with the agenda?' The reply came, 'If we are to be one body, we cannot leave any part of our burdens or of our blessings outside this room.' It turned out that they were completely right. Their sharing with one another has not only brought the members into a spirit of greater unity and fellowship, but it has brought within the direct concern of the Council things which are going on in industry and in the local community. Attention is no longer focused exclusively upon the activities of the branch, and the branch is more community centred. The minister's preaching has also been enriched by the knowledge which he gets through the Council's sharing.

This Council also arranged that, in respect of any matter of importance on the agenda, a Commission should be appointed to provide all members, a week ahead of the meeting, with a brief report. They commented, 'We are not intellectuals, and cannot analyse a situation or a problem immediately it is put to us. We must be given time to think things over, if we are to come to corporate and responsible decisions.' Here again the laymen were right. Now minister and laymen are experiencing real team-work together, and the minister finds himself helping this body of people to be God's local prophet, his evangelist, teacher, and servant – in a word, Christ's local body. No doubt God still has individual people he calls to be prophets or doctors, but ordinary ministers cannot be teachers of the world or servants of the local community. The minister's function is to serve the local congregation in such a way that the congregation itself can fulfil its responsibilities to the local community. The strength of the impact of a congregation on industry and the industrial community will largely depend, first of all, upon the attitude of its minister to the spiritual leadership of its lay leaders, and, next, upon the attitude of those lay leaders to their personal commitments and to their fellow members of the congregation and of the centre.[1]

It is our experience and practice that nobody should be appointed to the ruling body of the branch if he is not already committed to the service of the local community and to one or other activity of the centre. He must also be able to take an interest in the life of the community at large and of the centre in its different sections. There is a danger that members of a Council will only be committed within the centre; but a branch has more to do than merely to run a community centre! It is of the greatest importance to keep an eye on people, so that nobody overworks himself and everybody is helped to be active. Very often, in order to start working for others, a man does not need to be pushed, but rather to be helped to feel that he is capable of achieving something useful and can learn how to do it.

[1] Horst Symanowski, the originator of German industrial mission after World War II, speaks of the minister as the auxiliary of the laity.

To return to the members of the Council of a branch. Their attitude to ordinary members of the congregation and of the centre should be one of permanent consultation and spiritual support. In this field of responsibility, in most branches, the Annual Meeting plays a very important part.

In one branch, one year, the twenty members of the Council decided to go out, two by two, and interview all the seventy or eighty people who were running the different activities of the centre or taking responsibility in secular organizations. When this suggestion was first made, the warden said, 'You already complain of being overworked. How can you think of coping with all this extra visiting?' But eventually all members agreed that, 'the Lord wants us to listen to one another'. So they set out to do it, and did it; and interviewed the permanent staff as well. The warden was a little taken aback when members of the Council were deciding who would visit whom, and heard his name put down on the list of those to be visited, as well as on the list of the visitors. 'But after all, why not?' he asked himself. 'You are a member of a team, and it is in order to back you up spiritually that other members of the same team want to interview you.' All twenty Council members were visited, and did their visiting, helped by a questionnaire: 'Are you happy with what you are doing for others? Do you feel helped by the congregation? If you do not want to retain this responsibility, have you found somebody else to replace you? Have you got any comments or questions you would like the members of the centre to consider?'

One can well imagine the benefit which people, who usually do things for others, can get out of suddenly becoming persons for whom others are caring. It was most comforting. It also bound people more closely to one another. Each interviewer had to write a report with the help of the questionnaire. What was confidential was retained by the interviewer, and only the permanent staff were informed; but the Council as a whole received through these reports a lot of information not only about members' commitments but also about their views, their criticisms and their hopes about both their life from Monday to Friday and what they did in the centre.

Another year, another branch Council turned to the leaders of the twenty different activities of the centre and asked them to hand in, by a given date, a report stating the extent to which their activity had proclaimed Christ and his will for people. To what extent had they really been of benefit to ordinary people living and working in the local community? Had the plans made twelve months before been carried out, and had any future plan been made? What were, in their opinion, the two main issues which the branch would have to face in the coming year?

The leaders had been given a month's notice of the Council's intention. They discussed these searching questions, and handed in their reports for the Council to study. The Council found that a good deal had happened for which they could indeed be very grateful to the Lord; but they also expressed their opinion that: (i) there was too much complacency in some reports: (ii) among all leaders there was a feeling of being too heavily committed in the centre to have enough time to give to secular organizations. After two meetings and much laborious effort, the Council came out with what someone called a 'bombshell': it actually did cause some disturbance. The hundred most active people received a green document which began by stating: 'Let's imagine that next autumn our group of one hundred people is transferred to a similar working-class district of a large industrial city and has the disposal of more or less the same premises. We would have to make a new start, and ask ourselves what should be our priorities in the service of industry and of the community. That is precisely what we ought to be doing here next autumn.'

Then the green document enquired, 'What services do you render (or would you like to render) to the local community and industry? Are you already in contact with secular organizations, or would you wish to become responsible for establishing contact with them?' It next dealt with the sort of activities, in order of priority, which the centre ought to be providing for the industrial community, the children, the young people, the adults and the old people. At the Annual Meeting, people came with their copy of the green document, asked for supplementary information, and finished answering the questions.

The Council met again to study the final results, and it became clear that it would be possible to organize six or seven different teams to establish better contact with secular bodies (trade unions, the peace movement, political parties, etc.) and with neighbouring Protestant churches and the Roman Catholic parishes of the borough. It also appeared that priority should now be given, in the sphere of youth work, to teenagers rather than to children. The Children's Club would operate only once a week, instead of five or six times. Six young people of twenty or so volunteered to be trained as teenage club leaders; and a few adults undertook to make a careful survey of the teenage population of the borough, to see whether, with the younger leaders, their club might open most nights of the week. A sort of open club or café would function every Saturday afternoon, for adults to meet informally; and thirty people volunteered to be in charge in turns. A number of suggestions were made on what subjects should be dealt with in sermons, discussions, Bible studies, public meetings, and training conferences.

Who attends such an Annual Meeting? The meeting is

public and is advertised as such in the branch's magazine. Anybody interested enough in the general life of the branch is welcomed, whether he is a Christian or not. The majority are Christians; but there is a significance in the presence of non-Christians. It is a sign that the sons of God live in the midst of their nation, as Jesus and the apostles did. It also demonstrates that Christians do not form a closed shop, and do not allow themselves to think that they could live out the Gospel anywhere but right in the midst of the world, in the presence of and with some help from the non-churchgoers. That again is a truth we learn from Galilee. The presence of agnostics reminds those who have already answered Christ's call that they must be very grateful and full of joy; and that they must keep on asking for more spiritual wisdom and insight to know more of him (Ephesians 1.15-18). One by one, he adds more people to his body.

Before being officially accepted as church members during a service of worship, people must have stated privately that they have experienced personal fellowship with Christ, who has convinced them by his Spirit that he is alive and active today. They must have become regular worshippers, must have started making a serious offering of their earnings, and must have begun giving time to the service of others within the centre, in the local community, and at work. They will, of course, also have had several conversations with the minister.

All branches tend increasingly not to accept young people as church members under the age of seventeen or even eighteen. As Christine, a girl of sixteen, once said: 'If I said I was in love, I suppose you would not doubt the sincerity of my feelings; but you would disapprove of any official announcement until my fiancé and I were old enough to be sure that ours was the sort of love that could last a lifetime. My eldest brother was sincere at fifteen when he officially became a church member. Now he is twenty-one and he says he has given it up because he does not believe any more. He told me that the Church should have given him time to mature, and then perhaps this would never have happened.'

Christine and her brother, belonging to a non-church-going family, were expressing freely what numbers have told us, and were partly explaining why such a small number of first communicants (in some congregations not more than 10%) remain faithful to the Church and to their pledge to live with Christ and serve him.

For some time we have been painstakingly considering what to do, in face of the Protestant Church's general practice of having a two-year course of instruction for young communicants of thirteen, ending at the Easter when they are fifteen. Eventually the very simple but quite revolutionary realization came to us that the Sabbath and all other religious institutions were there for people's sake; the people were not there to fit into the institutional pattern. With the liberty given by the churches to the Mission, we are experimenting with a different discipline. Varying in form from year to year, youth Bible classes are held which last until the age of seventeen or eighteen. But, by the age of fifteen or sixteen, if young people ask for it (and few do), they are invited with no ceremonial at all to come up to the Lord's table; confirmation or baptism, however, will not take place until a couple of years later.

We are very grateful to the church that we are allowed to conduct such experiments. One branch has also, in the last few years, decided to allocate to young church members a Christian couple of their choice, to sponsor them in the Christian life as long as they wish. If the couple seems a suitable one, the Bible-class leader or the minister approaches them; usually they will gladly accept the privilege of tutoring the boy or girl, and will be introduced to their new responsibilities in a series of conversations. The couple will meet the parents, will invite the young member to visit them frequently, and will be at his disposal to listen to anything he may have on his mind and would like to speak about: they will also try to help him to correct his mistakes and receive God's absolution. This branch has about twenty people acting as tutors for about as many young people, and all are convinced that God has enriched them through this ministry which they have accepted.

If one wanted to sum up one's general impression of the 'young churches' of the branches of 'La Mission Populaire', the word 'to care' would at once come to mind; or better, 'to care corporately'. They care about God's love and his scheme for the world and its future; they care about industry and the industrial society, about the world at large and about the Church. Through corporate sharing, corporate responsibility and prayer, corporate work and pastoral care for one another and for the down-trodden of a harsh world, and through corporate action in the secular bodies of the community, they enter with joy into the great adventure in which Christ leads them, for the sake of men and to God's glory. Is this not the very purpose for which Christ wants to build up his servant Church?

10

The Mission and the Churches

THE days are over for 'La Mission Populaire' when the leaders and people of the branches usually had a purely negative attitude towards the traditional 'bourgeois' Protestant churches, and were extremely hostile to the Roman Catholics. Thanks to the work of the Holy Spirit in all churches, and in ourselves, 'La Mission Populaire' now attempts to be as much involved in the Church as it is in industrial society; and this involvement has become a part of the life of its branches.

Up to 1963, during the winter months, the St Nazaire branch of the Mission was responsible for La Baule. But in the summer-time, when upper-class people attended the church in this very expensive holiday resort, the responsibility was withdrawn from us. There was, one supposes, some suspicion in the mind of the Eglise Reformée, that preachers from the Mission might be too revolutionary. In 1963, however, at its request the Mission was left in charge of La Baule for the summer season, too, and the arrangement seems to have operated with God's blessing. Twice in July and twice in August, ecumenical Bible classes were organized in conjunction with the Roman Catholics, and dealt with such subjects as the use of leisure, and 'Who is my neighbour?' Each month, a party was taken to the neighbouring city of St Nazaire, ten miles away, visiting the shipyards and the rebuilt city, and meeting trade union militants, both Christians and agnostics, at the Mission centre. It has been very much appreciated by all parties concerned, and the leaders of the Mission are very grateful for this opportunity to minister to both sides in industry and build a temporary bridge for genuine encounters.

At the request of the Montbeliard Lutheran Synod, 'La Mission Populaire' has appointed an urban and industrial adviser to the forty churches of this highly industrialized small county, which provides the manpower for the Peugeot car works. This is the first appointment of an 'industrial adviser' in France. Our man does not have the opportunity of visiting people at work regularly, as British chaplains do, but the few times he has been allowed to meet people at the bench or in their office have led him to consider the possibility an immense asset. Not the least important thing is the fact that the person visited by the 'padre' is receiving him in his own world, and has the feeling that he is in a position to teach him something: at last the usual relation between minister and layman, i.e. teacher – pupil, is reversed, and the minister can be the assistant of the layman, who has to stand on his own feet at work. Our man has an opportunity to organize a certain number of groups who meet regularly: at present, three are concerned with gathering management together, two with foremen and superintendents, and several with shop-floor workers. The churches have been quite co-operative, and have sent lists of their members classified by industrial occupation. For all that, however, the reader should not think that the parish ministers all see the relevance of what is happening. All too often, their only question is still: 'Will this bring people into church?', and our man finds it difficult to, as he says, 'tread on the toes of forty colleagues' in interfering with 'their' parishioners.

One of the results of our man's work has been the appearance, in several industrial communities through the country, of a certain number of 'Equipes Ouvrières Protestantes'. These working-class groups are, of course, open to non-Protestants and to non-Christians. They meet regularly to study the challenges French industry brings to the man on the shop floor. They also meet to discuss the difficulties workers encounter in middle-class churches, and possibilities for their witness among their fellow-worshippers and their service to the Church at large.

Though once again the Mission's emphasis is on the Church's presence with the 'working man', the leaders of the Mission gladly welcome openings for serving other areas in industry and are grateful to the Lutheran Synod for this opportunity. Perhaps others will follow. In Lyons, the Lutheran Church and the Eglise Reformée have asked the Mission to take charge of a new housing estate of 6,000 flats, containing blocks of dwellings 350 yards long and seventeen storeys high. Premises were bought and transformed into a centre with the help of the Lutheran World Federation, and made over to the Mission. It was specifically laid down that if a congregation were born in this industrial community (and this has actually happened in the first two years' work), this congregation should not be given a denominational label for at least ten years, but should be in full communion with both denominations, and therefore be a sign of hope for Christian unity between the Lutheran and Reformed Churches.

The work, in Lyons as well as in Montbeliard, is under the authority of a local committee, whose members have been appointed by the Churches and the Mission in equal numbers. The Churches and the Mission finance the projects, but the Churches have the largest share in the financial burden to be carried.

Less spectacular, but just as useful and as well received, are the visits paid by staff members of the Mission to ordinary churches, theological colleges and ministers' fraternals, as well as the part they play on several committees of the National Churches and of the Protestant Federation, of which the Mission is a member. For example, the Mission was recently invited to take part in a consultation on the reform of the teaching of practical theology in Divinity Colleges. Several senior ministers of the Mission are also occasionally in charge of ordinands during their first year of pastoral service.

What are the relations of the Mission with the Roman Church?

Father Ernest, a Roman Catholic priest, walked into our centre one day to have a chat. He is now on the staff of the 'Mission de France', which is the successor in different ways to the worker-priest movement of which he was once a member. We first met when he was in contact with certain Muslim and French people who were opposing official policy during the Algerian war. At the time, the staff of 'La Mission Populaire' were also very much concerned in the same business. On this particular day, Father Ernest came up with an unexpected question. We were within a few weeks of the General Assembly of the World Council of Churches at New Delhi, and he asked me in his usual joking style, 'Georges, could you get me a ticket for New Delhi?' I laughed at him. 'I'm just an ordinary minister, and not in a position to do what you ask.' I went on to enquire from him, 'Why would you be interested in the World Council's General Assembly?' Father Ernest lit another cigarette. 'I'll tell you,' he said, and I knew he had something worth while to say. 'From the very beginning of my ministry as a worker priest, I have always been eager to find out what it means when we claim that Christ is the Light of the secular world. Is that not the theme of the Assembly? I am convinced that all the differences between our churches, important and dramatic as they are, should not and cannot stop us searching together for a better understanding of Jesus as the Light of the world, and for clearer vision of what we must do, if possible together, to be his witnesses and servants to fulfil his purpose for mankind.'

It was with a deep feeling of happiness that I listened to Father Ernest, and we would have rejoiced even more if we had known how many were going to share in our own ecumenical experience. We had been made brothers and would still remain so under the painful sting of the misunderstanding of many of our fellow Christians. It would not be honest to say nothing of their sufferings, the blow it was for us and our common anxiety about ecumenical relations.

Nuncio Roncalli! At a later stage he became a very different man when he was elected Pope and took the name of John XXIII. But when he was in Paris in the 'fifties as Pius XII's nuncio, he played a prominent part in the Pope's decision to attempt to stop the worker-priest experiment. This was a terrible blow to all Christians sharing the fate of the industrial communities, a terrible set-back that gave us the feeling that all the understanding that had painfully come about over the previous ten or fifteen years between Christians and the large agnostic majority of our communities was ruined. The bridge between the Churches and the working-classes was being smashed to pieces by the hierarchy of the main denomination at the request of some laymen and priests, reactionary in both the religious and the political realms. Our friends, our companions of service and witness, were being denied the right to be genuine workers and genuine Christians. We listened with an angry ear to all the nonsense about their moral and political behaviour. It was all right for the Church if a man was a teacher, a Conservative MP, a naval officer of high rank who had been ordered to open fire on Haiphong and start the Indo-China war. But to serve his mates on the shop-floor by letting himself be appointed a shop-steward was a great peril for the priest's spiritual balance and those he lived with! We admired those bishops who gave permission to some worker priests to go on working in their factories for a few years, against the official will of the Pope. We prayed for the very few who thought that they could not remain priests, and we prayed for those who, in silence, were preparing with the French hierarchy the birth of the admirable 'Mission de France'. After the crucifixion a sort of resurrection happened, and we also blessed the Lord for Pope John and the impulse he gave to his church. But we still welcome in our midst priests who feel that they cannot honestly remain Roman Catholics, and we go on co-operating, whenever possible, with those who do. We know very well that Christianity today is not divided only along denominational lines, and that it takes just as much spiritual love and Christian determination to endeavour to co-operate with some of our Protestant brothers.

Six Protestant churches have parishioners in the 11th arrondissement of Paris. At present, none have been willing to be involved with the local branch of the Mission in the service of the community alongside secular organizations. Out of the six Roman Catholic churches, at present only one is doing so. But today, some progress seems to be in sight. The Protestant churches have agreed to consider the question of birth control and the need to provide people with more advice on contraception and counselling on what it is to be husband and wife and to enter into responsible parenthood. A few members of one of the reluctant Roman Catholic parishes are about to join members of the branch of the Mission in starting a school for immigrant workers, eager to learn to read, write and count. This last positive step only came about after the Council of the branch had refused to go on praying for Christian Unity in a united service as the Vicar was still refusing all co-operation in the service of the community. The Vicar himself had said that he did not think it appropriate that Roman Catholics and Protestants should go on praying for Christian unity if the Protestants made it a condition that prayer should be followed by common action in the form of service to the community. But, as I have said, progress is now being made.

If 'La Mission Populaire' is working for a rapprochement between all churches, it is at the same time emphasizing that the path to unity is also the path of service to the urban and industrial society. There is a real danger, as we see things, that local churches may become primarily concerned with dogmatic and denominational differences, and may forget their common service to secular society and ordinary people. Thanks, however, to the work of the World Council of Churches, we are all reminded that the Gospel, and the very nature of the Church, imply worship, witness, service and unity at the local level; and that all these must be rooted in the teaching of the Scriptures and in Christ, with prayer.

It had been very beneficial to the Mission to have had long-established relationships with Christians and churches in Britain, the United States, Switzerland, and more recently in French-speaking African States, as well as with Germany and Czechoslovakia. It was through an invitation given by the Mission that Czech ministers renewed contact with the French Protestant churches in the early 1960s. It was rewarding to listen to what those Christians had to say about the witness of the Church in a secular and Marxist society. Members of the staff of the Mission have been and still are working with the Prague Peace Conference.

Some of the countries named above have a Committee of Friends of the Mission. For many years now, these Committees have faithfully supported the work in France by their prayers and their very welcome and necessary financial help. Even more important now is the part played by such Committees as the British Committee in the sharing of experience between those engaged in similar industrial mission enterprises. The British Committee is chaired by a Bishop of the Church of England, and contains members of the Church of Scotland and of all the main British denominations. It publishes a quarterly newsletter named after the founder of the Mission, 'The McAll News', recording what the Mission and the French churches are doing to relate the Church to industry and industrial communities.[1] It is now organizing an annual consultation for British and French ministers and laymen actively engaged in urban and industrial mission. Such a confrontation is often difficult, but always beneficial when it comes to discussing differences in approach to the Western type of industrial society and the theological implications of work and mission.

The workers of the Mission benefit from what is being attempted in Britain and elsewhere, through the reports brought back by those of the staff who spend some time travelling abroad. They also benefit from the material provided by the World Council of Churches, and from the endeavours of a growing number of French Christians to see 'the churches given to the world as God has given his Son to the world', to quote the Aix-en-Provence General Assembly of the Protestant Federation.

[1] *Address:* 22, The Gallop, Sutton, Surrey.

122

The Church and the World

A L L round the world, the industrial revolution and today's scientific and technical advances are challenging peoples and churches. There is increasing urbanization of different types. A working-class conscience has grown up, whether sustained by Marxism or not, which is generally secular in its outlook and contests the established order of society. New and quickly changing techniques are being introduced, making it necessary to provide the relevant educational facilities for children, young people and adults. All political systems are being challenged by the necessities of economic planning, involving technical decisions with political implications which parliaments still have the responsibility to control. There is increasing interdependence between larger and smaller countries, richer and poorer nations. One nation, or a group of nations sharing the same ideology, is fearful of others who face a different fate with a different philosophy. Each nation or group of nations is trying to influence, if not control, the others. All these aspects of modern life challenge all men and all churches. If Christ is the Light of mankind, to listen to his Word in the midst of any modern industrial society must make a world of a difference. If he is the Saviour, then the churches, and each local congregation, can play a very important part in helping their fellow-citizens to overcome the temptations which are the counterpart of man's new potentialities. They can act as salt, preserving this world from decay for the coming of a new, more glorious, world, of which many more are to become in advance the fortunate citizens.

It would appear that any church in any country ought to welcome an 'industrial mission', to help its congregations to enter with godspeed into this challenging adventure. If all countries are to be partly or essentially industrial, and therefore urban also, the question which nobody can seriously evade is: What does it mean to be a Christian, and what does it mean to be a Christian congregation, in an industrial and urban society? If each local congregation is to be missionary and live for the local community, how can such a church and its members meet God's challenge to them without answering this question?

National churches must not aim to have an 'industrial mission' in order to 'bring the workers into the pews' of the existing churches in their present patterns, or to set up working-class congregations. An 'industrial mission' should not be a substitute for the direct responsibility of churches situated in industrial communities. Nor does the Gospel invite us to segregate people into different congregations according to their class, any more than according to the colour of their skin. Our experience in 'La Mission Populaire' is that an 'industrial mission' should and can be *a movement in the Church for the world*, in order to help the Church and local congregations to be Christ's body in industrial society.

A movement? It must be an organization run by ordained ministers and qualified laymen appointed by the Church, with an independent structure, and only loosely tied to the traditional ecclesiastical organization. This will give it freedom to experiment in Christian ventures. Thus it may assist the Church to move to a better understanding of secular society and of the transformations through which

124

ordinary congregations will have to move, if they are to fulfil their responsibility of being Christ's body in industrial society, in the new economic structures of the future.

The Roman Catholic French experiment with worker priests and their present 'Mission de France', as well as our own 'Mission Populaire', show how important it is that industrial mission work should be interdenominational in action, ecumenical in attitude, and national in organization. As a number of events have shown, local experiments can be disbanded when there is no national organization to secure their continuity and adequate staffing. A national organization, while leaving a very large freedom for experimentation in each locality or region, also provides the indispensable framework through which branches can co-operate in research, both sociological and theological, and in the training of ministers and laymen.

The organized churches bear a spiritual responsibility towards 'industrial missions'. They must provide the necessary staff and the required financial support. They must encourage scholarship in such fields as theology, economics, and sociology, to help the Mission to an understanding both of industrial society and of God's Word for that society. Last, but not least, they must insist that local congregations should keep themselves informed about the work and support it with their prayers and their offerings.

There is also a responsibility which the 'industrial mission' bears towards the churches. What would be the use of experiments into the nature of Christ's Church in industrial society if the staff of the Mission did not give time to the organized Church, and did not get people from the branches to meet members of ordinary congregations? This is no easy venture. There is, unfortunately, a risk that some traditional Christians may be a stumbling-block in the path of people who are on the fringe of the Church. Did that not happen in

St Paul's time? Contacts with the people of the organized churches require time and prayer; but even more, there is the necessity for industrial mission workers to become 'bilingual'. For, in industrial mission, we learn to speak of religion in secular terms: we are trying to relate the Christian faith to secular issues which churchgoers and non-churchgoers have to meet week after week. That language, and that approach, are often quite alien to traditional Christians. We shall have to translate what we are accustomed to saying: we shall have to start where churchgoers are, exactly as we have felt compelled by God's Spirit to do in the case of the non-churchgoers in our industrial communities. Our 'lower nature' might well intervene here and try to induce us to think we could dispense with such a programme, perhaps because we would like to see traditional churches become outward-looking bodies, or perhaps just because we lose patience with our Christian brethren, who seldom see what difficulties some of their collective attitudes put in the way of our own witness. Here again Christ and his apostles give us the lead; and we can only admire and try to follow the love that always went with firmness when they spoke either to the Jewish Church or to the young Gentile churches about their 'getting off the rails'. Because of their 'lower nature', they were naturally tempted, just as our churches and religious organizations are today, to set up barriers between themselves and the world, and to develop a self-centred type of faith. But today we bless the Lord for the fruits which an increasing number of local churches and ecclesiastical authorities are bearing, and for the ever more fruitful relationships which are developing between the Mission, the French churches and the Church at large. The writer will be grateful if this book is of some help in fostering still further such relationships for God's glory and his service in our industrial society.